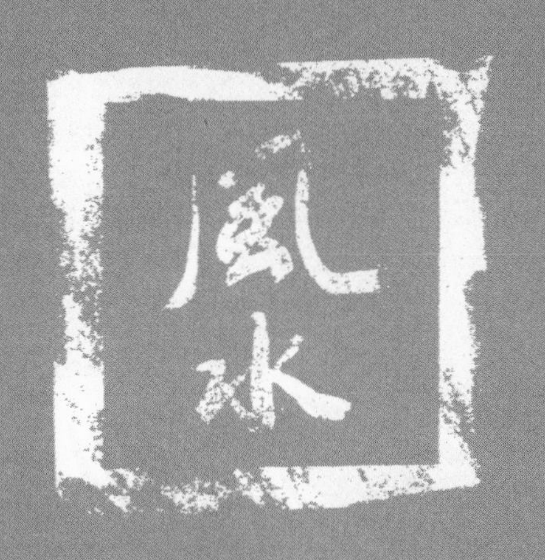
風水

GOOD VIBES

FENG SHUI

UNVEILING THE MYTHS

The healthy sceptic's guide that draws on the insights of contemporary physics. It questions and answers the ambiguities that others don't. Informed, you can decide for yourself.

First published in Great Britain in 2001 by Robson Books,
10 Blenheim Court, Brewery Road, London N7 9NY

A member of the Chrysalis Group plc

British Library Cataloguing in Publication Data
A catalogue record for this title is available from the British Library

ISBN 1 86105 426 1

PICTURE CREDITS

Unless otherwise credited below, all pictures were supplied by the author.

The publishers would like to thank the following for the use of their pictures:

Chinese paintings on pages 16, 39, 45, 68, 71, 85, 107, 173 supplied by The Gallery of China. Similar paintings can be purchased online at www.thegalleryofchina.com
Page 27 courtesy of Heather Angel/Natural Visions.
Page 91 courtesy of Werner Forman Archive.
page 99 AKG Photo London/Erich Lessing.
Chinese paintings on pages 21, 25(top), 31, 35, 47, 52, 94, 95(top), 108, 167, 175 courtesy of Chrysalis Images.
Paintings by Rosalyn Dexter on the following pages
25, 50, 95, 99, 103,104

Design and layout by Rosalyn Dexter

Printed and bound in Great Britain by Butler & Tanner Ltd, Frome and London

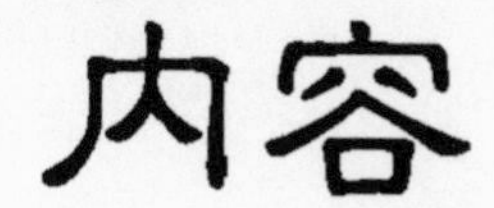

CONTENTS

ACKNOWLEDGEMENTS

My rather peripatetic and chaotic upbringing no doubt contributed to my desire to seek a passage in life that offered balance and ease. Along this journey I was fortunate to have many wonderful people touch my life.

Thank you Bernard and Mal for your unfailing support and faith.

Thank you Cathy and Linda for your time, your insight and your friendship.

To the many friends and family who reside in my silent gratitude . . . thank you.

Welcome

CHINA – THE MIDDLE KINGDOM

RUSSIA
MONGOLIA
Harbin
JAPAN
Beijing
KOREA
Seoul
Tokyo
CHINA
Kyoto
Nanjing
Shanghai
Wuhan

天體

Since Marco Polo's account of his years in the East, China has been viewed by the West as both inspiring and an 'other' world.

Known as the middle kingdom, it is the third largest country in the world. Its landmass is dominated by over 10,000 rivers and 1,000 mountains, wide open valleys, desert areas, narrow gorges and continual seasons of monsoons, cyclones and devastating floods. The constant changes in direction of the prevailing cold winds of Siberia and the moisture-laden warm ones from the Pacific cause extremes of cold in the winter and intense heat in the summer.

Now, if you had all of the above, you may also wish to know more about the elements and how to harness them beneficially.

That the Chinese chose to study the power and balance of the environment thousands of years ago . . . is no surprise.

That they should call it FENG SHUI meaning
WIND AND WATER,
also does not come as a surprise . . .

了解

In the early part of last century Einstein, Heisenberg and many other leading scientists were grappling with the new science of quantum physics. It was breaking all the previously conceived rules and turning classical physics on its head. It proposed that everything in our world exists as dynamic oscillating energy — VIBRATION.

From their work, and from more recent scientific studies, we have come to understand that we as individuals are a composite of particles vibrating at a particular frequency, our own unique frequency discerning and separating us from the vibrational frequency of say, a wall, a table, a chair, the food we eat, heat, light, even the floor beneath our feet.

Us — the universe and all there is — vibration.

With this understanding — that we and all things are vibrations interacting with, and affecting each other, then surely an environment having . . . GOOD VIBES takes on a whole other meaning.

. . . and if there were an instructive way to determine a good vibe we just might want to know about it!

Interestingly enough, thousands of years ago, without access to any sophisticated technology, the Chinese proposed a similar concept with their analysis of the universe. They proposed that our universe comprised matter and energy and that these were interacting and interchangeable — our inner and outer worlds constantly affecting each other.

— chi — matter — chi

—matter — energy — matter

They called the way of the natural world 'The Tao' and their analysis of it Feng Shui.

• • •

Feng Shui has had a curious birth into our Western mindset: two rather foreign-sounding words that seem to conjure up this image of an 'other' world. Before I enter into a dissertation on the subject, I would like to cite some interesting facts that may help us appreciate the genius of this ancient culture and illuminate some of its intuitive insights into numbers, numerology and the esoteric, all of which contemporary society and science are only just beginning to embrace.

- The Chinese had a reverence for nature and a desire to understand the 'way of the natural world'. They recognised in ancient times – as our scientists do today – numerical patterns in nature, and believed that mathematics was at the core of creation.

- Back in the second century the Chinese were working with the concept of binary numbers, numbers which today are the basic language code of our computers. This was 1,500 years before the German physicist Leibniz came up with a formula for binary numbers as we know them today.

- These ancients calculated the ratio of the circumference of a circle to its diameter, 'pi', via algebraic gymnastics. Archimedes, who is considered one of the four great founding fathers of Western science alongside Galileo, Newton and Einstein didn't uncover this for another 700 years. 'Pi' is now used in equations for contemporary physics to describe subatomic particles.

- These Eastern sages observed that in life there were chance events that happened and they went as far as trying to understand and then predict them in a formulaic manner. To access the probability of these chance events happening in a certain time frame, they used numerology.

- Millennia later Werner Heisenberg proposed the 'uncertainty principle' which stated:

> There is after all some spontaneity in the physical world in the sense that not every event is determined by previous events.

- The ancient Chinese believed numbers were the basic code of our world. Physics, the science of our physical world, uses mathematics as its language:
vibrations – temporal patterns – are expressed as a number.

- Edward De Bono, one of the great lateral thinkers of our time, is currently working with the idea that numerical codes could become more vital in the future than our multifarious languages. He is proposing an international method of learning communication based on numbers and believes that coding information with numbers would break down the language barrier set by the need to translate inter-culturally.

Are we, and were they, tapping a far greater universal truth?
It does make one curious . . .

I hope !

So let us look back 4,000 years to China where they lived life based on intuited philosophical theories.

The Chinese believed the universe was self generating and that it gave birth to itself. Within this universe we were considered to be a microcosm of its macrocosm, with continual interaction between us. Observing the natural forces, they determined that there was a natural order to our universe based on the duality of all things. This natural order they believed to be guided and charged by two forces — Yin and Yang. Two forces shaping our world and everything in it.

Yin and Yang represent opposing qualities:

Yin is female	Yang is male
Yin is restful	Yang is active
Yin even	Yang odd
Contracting	Expanding
dark	light

Yang energy descends from the heavens
Yin energy ascends from the earth

Yin is night Yang is day

隆而不殺物無盛而不
滿則微崇猶塵積替

Yin and Yang — one is inseparable from the other as each inherently has a spark of the opposite. There is no day without night, for even as the day rests towards sunset it holds a spark of the expectant sunrise. This is illustrated in the Taiji symbol opposite representing wholeness and perpetual change.

The dynamic duality of these two primal energies, Yin and Yang, created our universe. A more familiar model for this dynamic duality is that of man and woman. We were born from this same unifying principle through the ultimate expression of life longing for itself. The mechanism used was humanity's own and conscious unifying force, the one that sets the creation of mankind in motion: ORGASM.

That tenuous link between man and woman, the moment where leaving Yang the potential for new life enters Yin. A Yang trajectory bridge, literally, from one external organism into a completely separate one. Unifying in an explosive pact with creation, where Yang chromosome xy merges with Yin chromosome xx to create: us.

I use this example to illustrate my point on a human-sized scale, so that we don't distract to the macro view of creation out there. Out there can seem so 'other than ourselves', so other world.

Orgasm — the power of the word alone — even in this 21st century we still tend to say it in hushed tones. Yet without the physical unifying bridge this dynamic moment creates, we wouldn't be here.

The act itself is so referenced in Taoist symbolism, male representing Yang-Heaven and female representing Yin-Earth. As in . . .

'Did the Earth move for you?' or 'It was Heaven!'

The experience itself conjures up metaphors of universal proportions . . . a place where heaven meets earth and unifies, becoming one with . . . I suppose CREATION . . . the big one. No one really knows how we got here; was creation a cosmic orgasm of sorts . . . what science calls the Big Bang!

愛

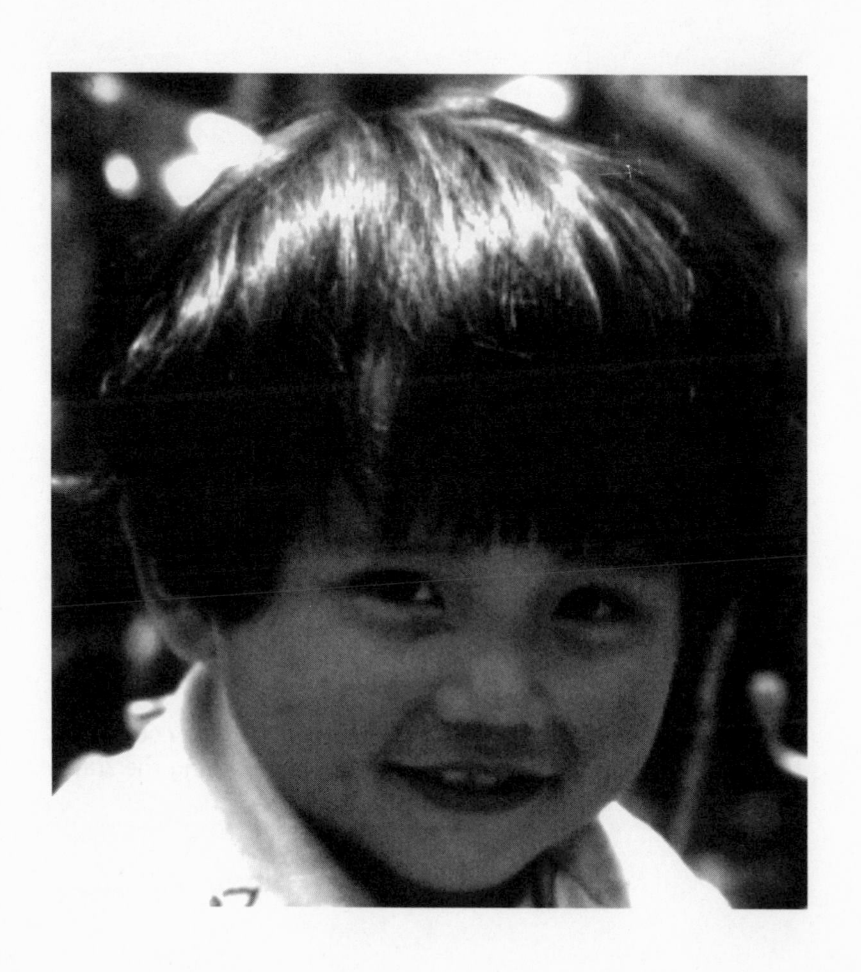

The ancients did not base their analysis of the natural world on any religious belief system, though there are many parallels with various biblical stories.

An obvious parallel with Yin and Yang is the story of Adam and Eve, as original male and female.

Adam and Eve were supposedly condemned for their original sin. Rather curiously, the study of Chinese history and its language is called 'SINology'.

Einstein and Heisenberg – Adam and Eve – Yin and Yang

The rational – the mythical and the intuitive

Maybe if we had evolved De Bono's proposed number codes way back, we would more easily see that we are all saying the same thing within our own terms of reference.

呼吸

People ask: why the popularity for Feng Shui now?

We are entering a time when the rational is meeting synergistically with the resurrecting intuitive, triggering an evolution of sorts.

THAT FOUR LETTER

'F'

WORD

AND

THAT FOUR LETTER

'ς'

WORD

They just keep popping up
and won't leave us alone.

Feng Shui

風水中心

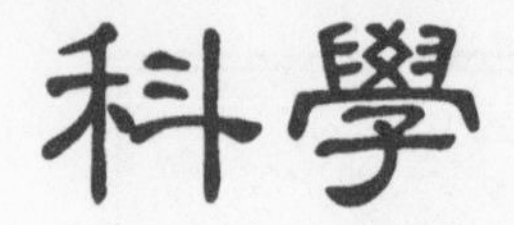

The words ‘Feng Shui’ literally mean ‘wind and water’.

Feng Shui’s classical origins were based on observation and an intuited understanding of the energy meridians of the cosmos formed from a protracted study of the environment's composite elements and their interaction with each other, inclusive of the human element. Its origin was not based in superstition. Those individuals over the centuries who have proposed a more superstitious context were possibly speaking from their own sense of powers beyond their ken. This has fuelled current Western scepticism because some exponents of Feng Shui and a few of the popular books have treated it like magic. But there is no magic at play here, just unfolding intelligent information. Information that new physics is starting to give names to, and so, at some point, acceptability will no doubt follow.

But, for the moment, Feng Shui seems to be just beyond what our rational mind and less-than mystical science can accept. Any scepticism surrounding Feng Shui though is in good company. The sixteenth-century astronomer and physicist Galileo — one of the the founding fathers of modern science — was considered a heretic by the Catholic Church for supporting the theory that the earth moved around the sun.

Columbus was ridiculed for suggesting the earth was round.

Today we can switch on a battery-powered radio, and from thin air sound is formed, i.e. there is no visible power source. If a hundred years ago I had suggested this I would have been called crazy.

What I am trying to suggest here is that we really don't know it all. In fact, the radio alone makes the apparent magic of Feng Shui seem pretty pedestrian.

I was my own healthy sceptic as I investigated the territory many, many years ago. Though not a follower of trends by nature, I allowed myself a curiosity when I sensed a mirroring of fine ergonomics inherent to Feng Shui's principles, and I was astute enough to recognise the spark it created in the work of some less-than-inspired designers.

It can be easy for the rational world to make light of something so unfamiliar, especially when we learn of numerology and that the star positions at our dates of birth are taken into consideration. Some people resist because it seems so intangible. Considering some of the advanced concepts these ancient sages were uncovering thousands of years earlier, without our sophisticated technology, it may be worth considering that their observation of planetary influence has some value.

After all, we now know that the moon affects the tide and since we are 60 per cent water, there is a strong possibility it affects us. Most of us have heard the term lunatic. Without the sun where would we be? The sun is a star and the moon is a planet.

So Feng Shui . . . Fact, Fad or Fui . . ?

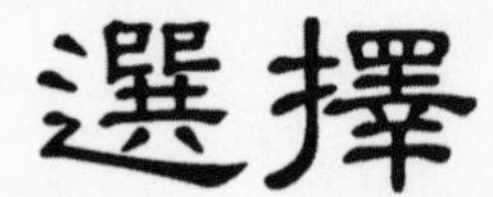

There are many differing views purported inside and outside of the profession. As I progressed in my studies, my inquisitive and logical mind was doing summersaults around the contradictory statements expressed by the different Feng Shui schools and masters.

Some teachers were getting students to chant blessings. That's more about prayer and space clearing – totally valid in of themselves – but not Feng Shui as I was understanding it. Feng Shui was never meant to be a religion. It evolved centuries before Taoism and Buddhism. Its only reference to the Tao is in its semantics. Tao meaning . . . 'the way of the natural world'.

If clients choose to add their own spiritual beliefs, I feel that is their right and privilege, and if it is meaningful to them, it may even enhance the resulting analysis. I am not going to ignore the incredible power of the mind and its ability to create a reality.

So how can we discern?

Most of you have possibly seen or heard about the murder-mystery movie that was filmed as seen through the eyes of three different people. The same crime with three completely different perspectives, each person convinced that their perspective was the way it was. Their views were so different it was hard to believe they could possibly have been describing the same scene.

So?

Well, what I learned as I observed and questioned Feng Shui's different practices was that it is certainly a source of information that can enhance one's life but not, as popularly believed, by moving a sofa or placing three goldfish in the southeast. It seems some less-than-inspired individuals were adding their own curves to its original genius. I wanted to discern and learn from the original – if I could!

I studied, discussed, argued – I had disappeared off the face of the planet as far as most of my contemporaries were concerned and I stopped consulting for a while. I couldn't, with a good conscience, advise clients until I felt clearer. Sometimes there is an advantage and an honesty in saying I don't know – that may be so in a philosophy class but not when one is charging a fee! I realised my clients looked to me as a 'sort of expert' . . . what I was now fast becoming was an expert in questioning.

My curiosity led me on a most amazing journey.

My conclusion . . .

The ancients really had it sussed — I was fascinated.

In a territory such as this there are few,
I KNOWs
but what there is, is information.

With some of this information, I would like to take you on
a journey — East.

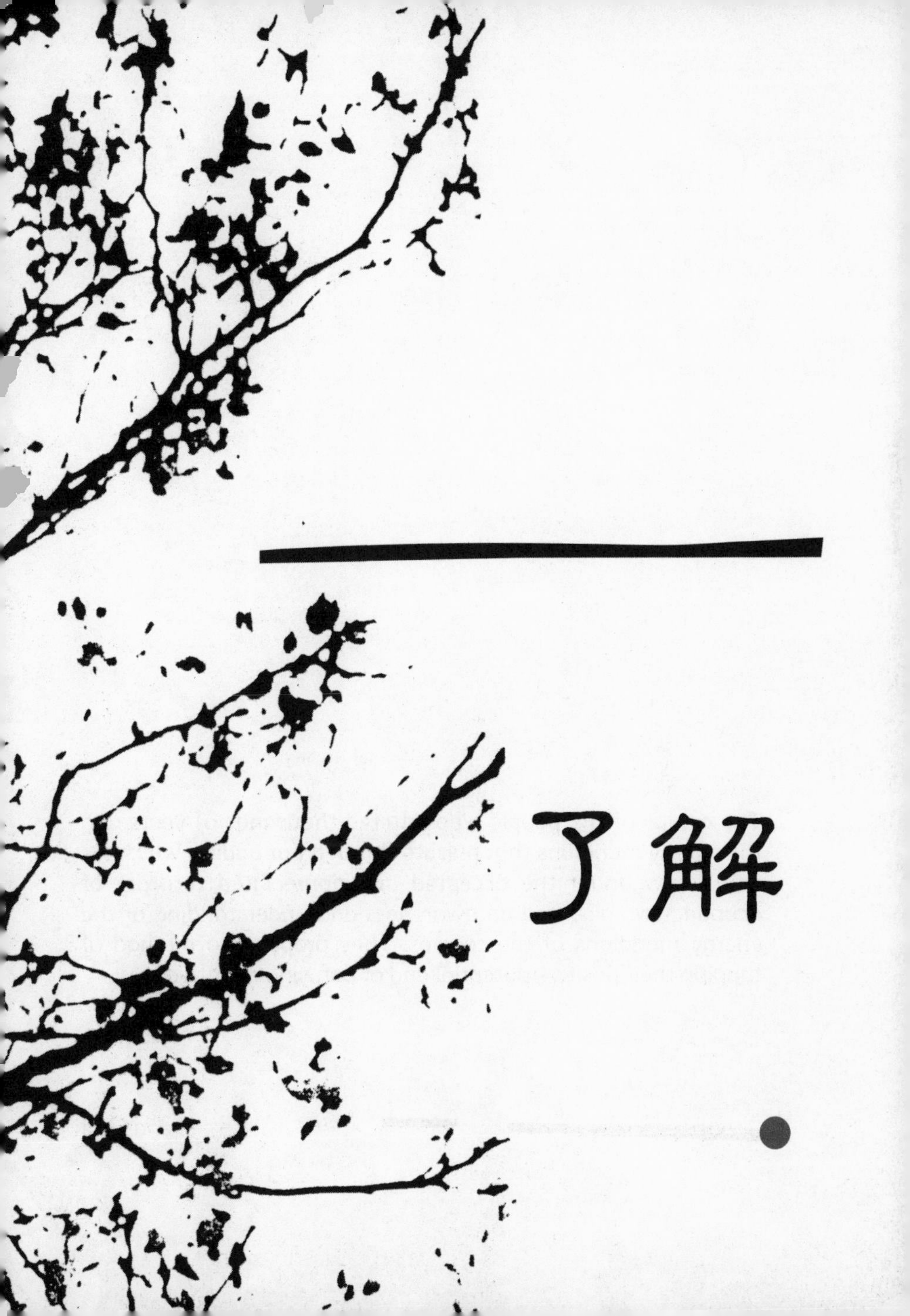

一

了解

The genius of the people who intuited thousands of years ago the energy meridians that pulsate through our bodies, which we now know under the accepted and appreciated territory of acupuncture, also had an awareness and understanding of the energy meridians of the cosmos. They proposed a method of tapping their positive potential and of defusing negative flow.

Feng Shui

心靈

THE DOORWAY TO INTELLIGENT DESIGN

The Chinese see us and the planet as an organic whole.

They regard the earth as a living organism much like our body is. As we have veins running through our body, they believe the earth has veins or channels too, mythically called 'the veins of the dragon'. The point at which these channels converge are considered to be auspicious sites. Insightful analysis of the landscape can ascertain the location of this bountiful place and that was the Feng Shui master's role. He used a combination of information and intuition to discriminate the degree to which a site was auspicious or not. The more finely tuned his intuition, the better his reading of a site.

The Chinese have a great reverence for the memory of their ancestors so initially Feng Shui was used for the siting of graves. As the centuries unfolded, their observations and analysis were extended into the siting and orientation of buildings on the landmass, their internal layout and then eventually to the design of whole cities.

There are many different schools of Feng Shui and discerning the original or best is not a clear route.

I chose and present here what is called Traditional Feng Shui. This is a combination of The form/landscape school and applied compass school. These two schools were merged at the beginning of the twentieth century to this form. It is the form most often used in both the East and West today. The concept of integrating the compass school with the form school came from the Chinese belief that each orientation of the magnetic forcefield accorded different qualities, and that each of us responds to those orientations differently. Our vibration interacts with the vibration of the different orientations. The ancient sages viewed this as our Chi interacting with the Chi of the environment . . . Chi being life's vital force. The result of this on a more tangible level is how and why each of us feels different in different environments . . .

The Form/Landscape School

Here the intention is to harness the auspicious Chi of the earth via its contours, location and waterways in relation to a building. Some of its references beyond Yin, Yang and the elements are cloaked in symbolic representations of the four spheres of heaven. These stellar constellations were given the names of the four celestial animals, the black turtle, the green dragon, the white tiger and the red phoenix. It was mythically believed that these ruled the four corners of the earth, north-south-east-west. The form school defines the landscape union of the Yin white tiger and the Yang green dragon, where they meet is considered to be the most auspicious location as it is symbolic of them mating. The popular name for this configuration is the Armchair Formation.

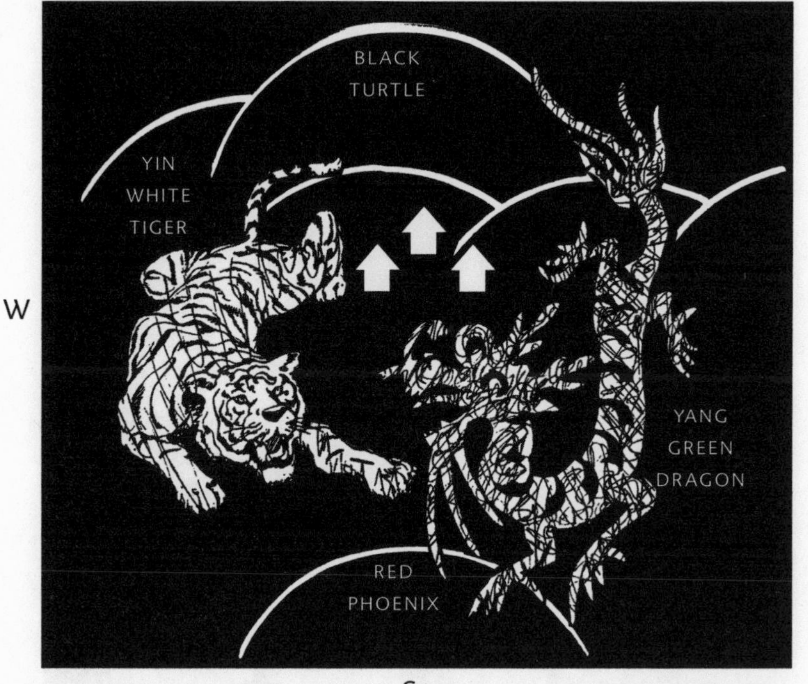

The four celestial animals represent four types of landform and location. Protection at the back and ideally north is provided by the turtle. At the sides the tiger is higher than the dragon, with a view of the territory to the front . The phoenix acts like a footrest.

The ideal is that the landscape should shelter you like a comfortable armchair. The perfect place to build a home would be nestled in the middle.

In contemporary landscape environments, tall trees or high rise blocks sheltering you from the rear represent turtle, buildings either side represent tiger and dragon.

古

Developing along side the form/landscape school was the compass school, which uses the eight-sided Pa Kua and its trigrams. This adopts a more mathematical approach with applied Chinese astrology, numerology and of course the magnetic forcefield for orientation.

It is believed that by discerning and then aligning with one's own personal best directions in a given environment, one's personal Chi may be harmoniously aligned with the Chi of the environment. Here one's date of birth is used to discern the orientations that are most beneficial for an individual. It is at this point, as I alluded to earlier, that some sceptics resist because it all sounds too unfamiliar, not logical enough.

For aeons many cultures have talked of the influence of the stars and, interestingly, it was the Chinese who were the first to develop an instrument for observing them. This was eleven centuries before anyone else, having already revealed their genius by inventing the compass. The West measured celestial positions with respect to the sun's path in the sky (ecliptic), the Chinese focused theirs on the celestial pole and the celestial equator. Guess what? The Chinese method was adopted in Europe in the sixteenth century. It just might be that those sages knew a thing or two.

I mentioned earlier that the Chinese were interested in numerology, codyfying information and in the synchronistic patterns of things and events. They believed numbers were the key to the way of our natural world and to unlocking its hidden wisdom. They believed unlocking this wisdom would enable them to harness the invisible forces governing the balance between heaven and earth.

THE INSPIRATION OF THE TURTLE

Legend has it that about 4,000 years ago a great sage was sitting on the banks of the Lo River meditating and ruminating on the workings of the Universe, when a turtle emerged from the water. As he was contemplating the splendour of its shell he noticed an unusual pattern of black and white markings. He was intrigued by their symmetry as the markings numerically added up to 15 in all directions. In a flash of inspiration the Universe – its workings inclusive of humanity, were revealed to him – he 'connected-the-dots' so to speak.

The Loshu Grid

4	9	2
3	5	7
8	1	6

The Loshu markings numerically added up to 15 in all directions.

In the grid you will notice that all the opposite numbers add up to 10.

2+8 = 10
4+6 = 10
3+7 = 10
9+1 = 10

If one adds together all the odd numbers around the centre = 20
And if one adds together all the even numbers = 20

So began the ancients' observation and research into man and his environment.

Their desire was to evolve a practice that they believed would serve humanity in a life-enhancing way. The underlying theory was of a natural order to our world. Within this we were a microcosm of its macrocosm, our inner and outer worlds continually interacting with each other, charged by the two forces – Yang and Yin

They believed Yang energy descended
from the Heavens – becoming more concentrated

and Yin energy ascended from the Earth –
rising and diffusing

Active Yang — Passive Yin
opposing yet complementing each other as:

male	female
heaven	earth
expansion	contraction
odd	even
hot	cold
light	dark
movement	stillness

A walk in the sunlight reveals the
light creating its opposite . . . shadow

A duality shaping everything in our world.

outer	inner
up	down
in	out
high	low
hard	soft
permeable	impervious

A precursor to Einstein's theory of relativity —
there is no here without there !

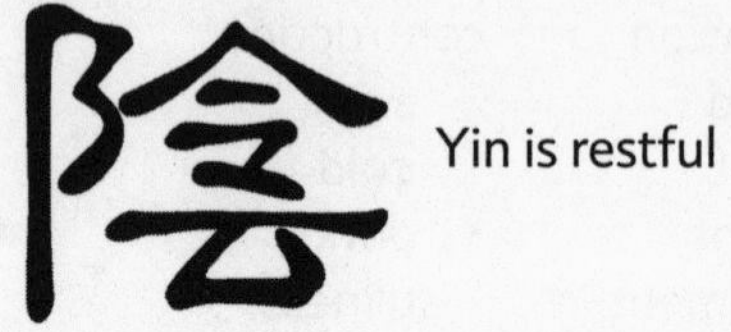
陰
Yin is restful

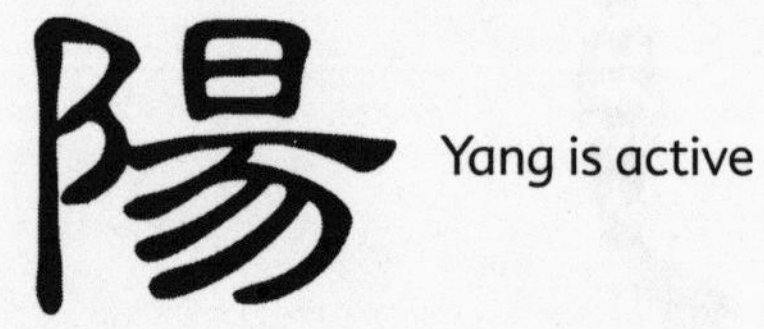
陽
Yang is active

These ancient sages, the equivalent of our scientists today – proposed that the universe comprised of matter and energy and that these were interchangeable.

Energy – Matter – Energy   Chi – Matter – Chi

The unifyng force Chi condensing into matter, shaping our world and everything in it . . .
presenting as the basic elements
WOOD – FIRE – EARTH – METAL – WATER

These elements, believed to be the basis for all living things, were continually interacting with each other in what were called THE FIVE STAGES OF CHANGE.

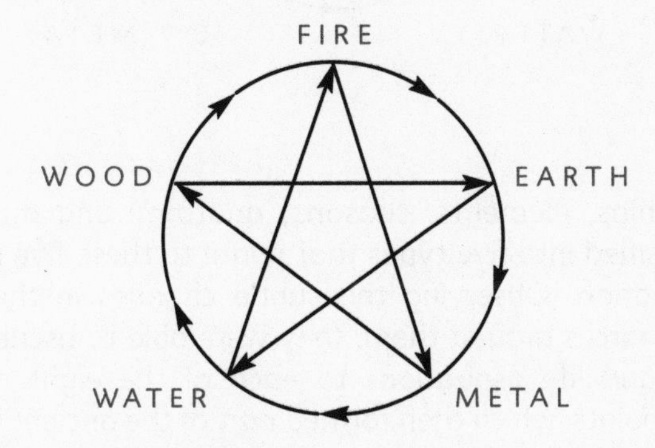

They were called THE FIVE STAGES OF CHANGE because there was constant transformation occurring.

Working with the laws of Yin and Yang and analysing these five stages of change, numerical value was ascribed to each stage.

This is also called the star cycle.

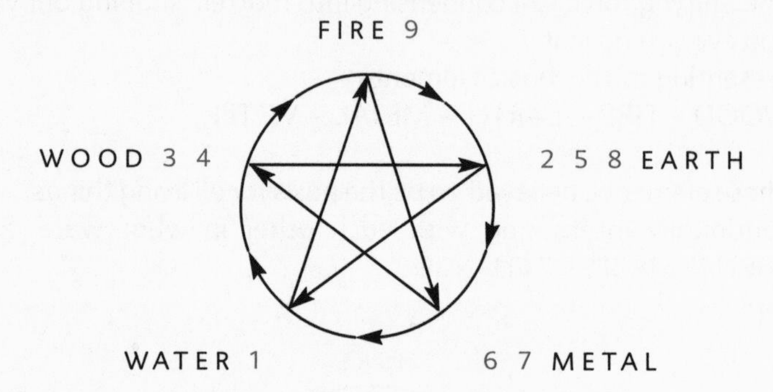

Relationships, elements, seasons, anatomy and much more were classified into five types that relate to these five phases of transformation. Observing the subtle changes in the electro-magnetic forces around them, they were able to ascribe certain qualities and life aspirations to each of the eight numbered compass points, which then formed part of the ancient Pa Kua.

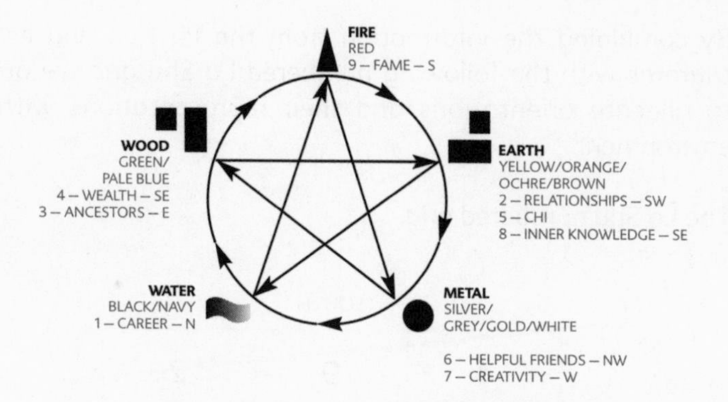

'Pa' means 'eight','Kua' means 'trigram'

The 'Pa Kua' - 'eight trigrams'

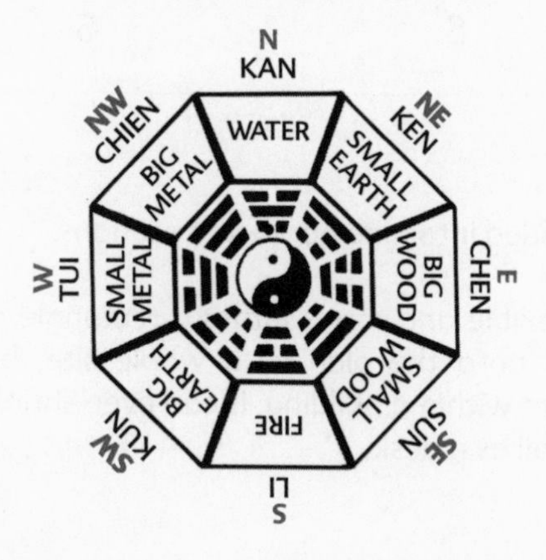

This is the early heaven sequence for Yang living environments, as opposed to late heaven for Yin grave sites.

Finding a balance between the constantly alternating Yin and Yang qualities is the challenge in Feng Shui.

By combining the information from the Pa Kua and its eight trigrams with the following numbered Lo Shu grid we are able to allocate orientations and their representations within an environment.

The Lo Shu numbered grid.

SOUTH

EAST	4	9	2	WEST
	3	5	7	
	8	1	6	

NORTH

The grid is divided into nine numbered sections.

This grid is flexible and forms either a rectangle or square. It is superimposed onto the plan of a whole site, building, or an individual room within a building. It can even shrink to work on a surface as small as a desk.

Before applying the information from the Pa Kua you simply draw a layout of your environment, superimpose the grid, and then align the numbers of the grid with the orientation of your site, building or room etc. using a compass.

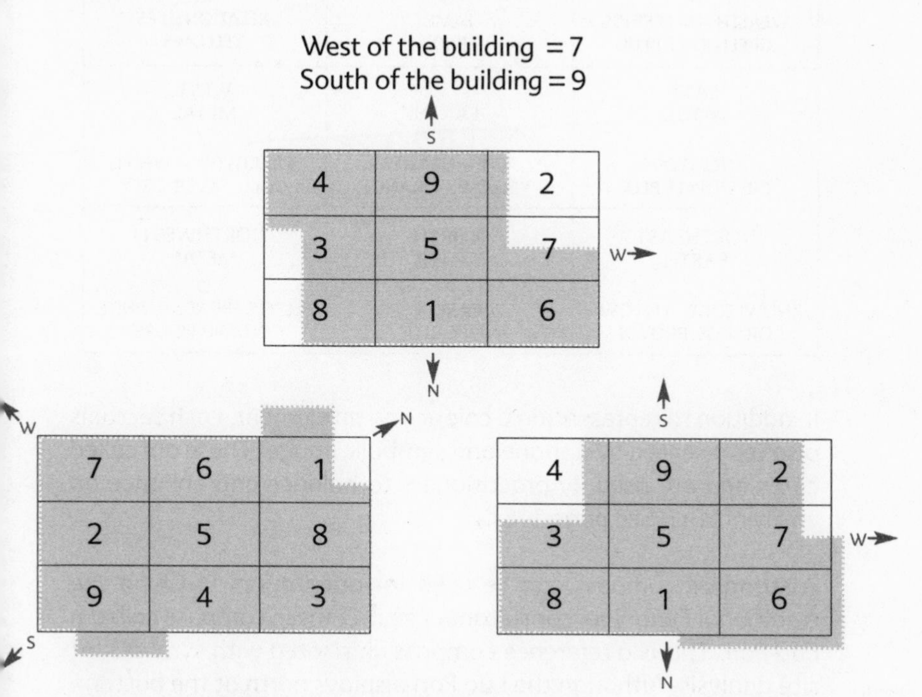

If there are different levels to the building, each succeeding floor is similarly divided into nine sections.

The importance of the square originates from the ancient Chinese belief that the heavens were represented by a sphere and the earth by a square, their perfect symetry representing wholeness.

The information from the Pa Kua is added to this grid.

SOUTHEAST WOOD 4 WEALTH – BLESSINGS GREEN, PALE BLUE	SOUTH FIRE 9 FAME RED	SOUTHWEST EARTH 2 RELATIONSHIPS YELLOWS
EAST WOOD 3 ANCESTORS GREEN, PALE BLUE	EARTH 5 CHI – HEALTH YELLOWS, ORANGE	WEST METAL 7 CREATIVITY – WHITE, GOLD, SILVER, GREY
NORTHEAST EARTH 8 KNOWLEDGE –YELLOWS, ORANGE, BROWN	NORTH WATER 1 CAREER NAVY/BLUE	NORTHWEST METAL 6 HELPFUL FRIENDS – WHITE, GOLD, SILVER, GREY

In addition to representing a colour and an element, each sector is also represented by a shape and symbolic image. These are called cures and are used by practitioners to balance and enhance an environment (See page 145).

A standard compass can be used for orientation. In China the traditional Feng Shui consultants use a Chinese compass called a Luo Pan. This is a reference compass illustrated with symbols for site analysis. Although the Luo Pan displays north at the bottom, this is still magnetic north.

Various electrical appliances and objects made of steel or iron can distort the compass reading, so walk around your building until a reading is consistent in several places before applying the reading to the grid.

ASCERTAINING YOUR PREFERRED DIRECTIONS: **for the compass school you need to identify your Kua number from the following chart.**

Despite being born in the same year, you will notice that males and females have different Kua numbers. This is because Chinese philosophy views them as opposites. The Chinese use the lunar calendar, reflecting the inner man.

YEAR OF BIRTH	NEW YEAR STARTS	KUA NUMBER MALE	FEMALE	ANIMAL	ELEMENT
1928	23 JAN	9	6	DRAGON	EARTH
1929	10 FEB	8	7	SNAKE	EARTH
1930	30 JAN	7	8	HORSE	METAL
1931	17 FEB	6	9	SHEEP	METAL
1932	6 FEB	5	1	MONKEY	WATER
1933	26 JAN	4	2	ROOSTER	WATER
1934	14 FEB	3	3	DOG	WOOD
1935	4 FEB	2	4	PIG	WOOD
1936	24 JAN	1	5	RAT	FIRE
1937	11 FEB	9	6	OX	FIRE
1938	31 JAN	8	7	TIGER	EARTH
1939	19 FEB	7	8	RABBIT	EARTH
1940	8 FEB	6	9	DRAGON	METAL
1941	27 JAN	5	1	SNAKE	METAL
1942	15 FEB	4	2	HORSE	WATER
1943	5 FEB	3	3	SHEEP	WATER
1944	25 JAN	2	4	MONKEY	WOOD
1945	13 JAN	1	5	ROOSTER	WOOD
1946	2 FEB	9	6	DOG	FIRE
1947	22 JAN	8	7	PIG	FIRE
1948	10 FEB	7	8	RAT	EARTH
1949	29 JAN	6	9	OX	EARTH
1950	17 FEB	5	1	TIGER	METAL
1951	6 FEB	4	2	RABBIT	METAL
1952	27 JAN	3	3	DRAGON	WATER
1953	14 JAN	2	4	SNAKE	WATER
1954	3 FEB	1	5	HORSE	WOOD
1955	24 JAN	9	6	SHEEP	WOOD
1956	12 JAN	8	7	MONKEY	FIRE
1957	31 JAN	7	8	ROOSTER	FIRE
1958	18 FEB	6	9	DOG	EARTH
1959	8 FEB	5	1	PIG	EARTH
1960	28 JAN	4	2	RAT	METAL
1961	15 FEB	3	3	OX	METAL
1962	5 FEB	2	4	TIGER	WATER
1963	25 JAN	1	5	RABBIT	WATER
1964	1 FEB	9	6	DRAGON	WOOD
1965	2 FEB	8	7	SNAKE	WOOD
1966	21 JAN	7	8	HORSE	FIRE
1967	9 FEB	6	9	SHEEP	FIRE
1968	31 JAN	5	1	MONKEY	EARTH
1969	17 FEB	4	2	ROOSTER	EARTH
1970	6 FEB	3	3	DOG	METAL
1971	27 JAN	2	4	PIG	METAL
1972	16 JAN	1	5	RAT	WATER
1973	3 JAN	9	6	OX	WATER
1974	23 JAN	8	7	TIGER	WOOD
1975	11 FEB	7	8	RABBIT	WOOD
1976	31 JAN	6	9	DRAGON	FIRE
1977	18 FEB	5	1	SNAKE	FIRE
1978	7 FEB	4	2	HORSE	EARTH
1979	28 JAN	3	3	SHEEP	EARTH
1980	16 FEB	2	4	MONKEY	METAL
1981	5 FEB	1	5	ROOSTER	METAL
1982	25 JAN	9	6	DOG	WATER
1983	13 FEB	8	7	PIG	WATER
1984	2 FEB	7	8	RAT	WOOD
1985	20 FEB	6	9	OX	WOOD
1986	9 FEB	5	1	TIGER	FIRE
1987	29 JAN	4	2	RABBIT	FIRE
1988	17 FEB	3	3	DRAGON	EARTH
1989	6 FEB	2	4	SNAKE	EARTH
1990	27 JAN	1	5	HORSE	METAL
1991	15 FEB	9	6	SHEEP	METAL
1992	4 FEB	8	7	MONKEY	WATER
1993	23 JAN	7	8	ROOSTER	WATER
1994	10 FEB	6	9	DOG	WOOD
1995	31 JAN	5	1	PIG	WOOD
1996	19 FEB	4	2	RAT	FIRE
1997	7 FEB	3	3	OX	FIRE
1998	28 JAN	2	4	TIGER	EARTH
1999	16 FEB	1	5	RABBIT	EARTH
2000	5 FEB	9	6	DRAGON	METAL
2001	24 JAN	8	7	SNAKE	METAL
2002	12 FEB	7	8	HORSE	WATER
2003	1 FEB	6	9	SHEEP	WATER
2004	22 JAN	5	1	MONKEY	WOOD
2005	9 FEB	4	2	ROOSTER	WOOD
2006	29 JAN	3	3	DOG	FIRE
2007	18 FEB	2	4	PIG	FIRE

To calculate further into the millennium simply follow the repetition of the cycles.

Having ascertained your Kua number, use the chart below to identify your preferred order of compass directions. These are listed in descending order starting with the most beneficial.

	M/F	M/F	M/F	M/F	M	F	M/F	M/F	M/F	M/F
KUA NUMBER	1	2	3	4	5	5	6	7	8	9
1ST	SE	NE	S	N	NE	SW	W	NW	SW	E
2ND	E	W	N	S	W	NW	NE	SW	NW	SE
3RD	S	NW	SE	E	NW	W	SW	NE	W	N
4TH	N	SW	E	SE	SW	NE	NW	W	NE	S
5TH	W	E	SW	NW	E	S	SE	N	S	NE
6TH	NE	SE	NW	SW	SE	N	E	S	N	W
7TH	NW	S	NE	W	S	E	N	SE	E	SW
8TH	SW	N	W	NE	N	SE	S	E	SE	NW

M=MALE F=FEMALE

In their order as listed, the first four directions bring slightly different kinds of benefit, but all are very supportive.

The 1st is for SUCCESS

The 2nd is HEALTH

The 3rd is FAMILY HARMONY

The 4th is GENERAL GOOD LUCK

Direction is the **alignment** or **way** you are facing or sleeping in any situation (the direction the crown of your head is pointing as you sleep).
Location is relative to the grid and is the position **where** you are.

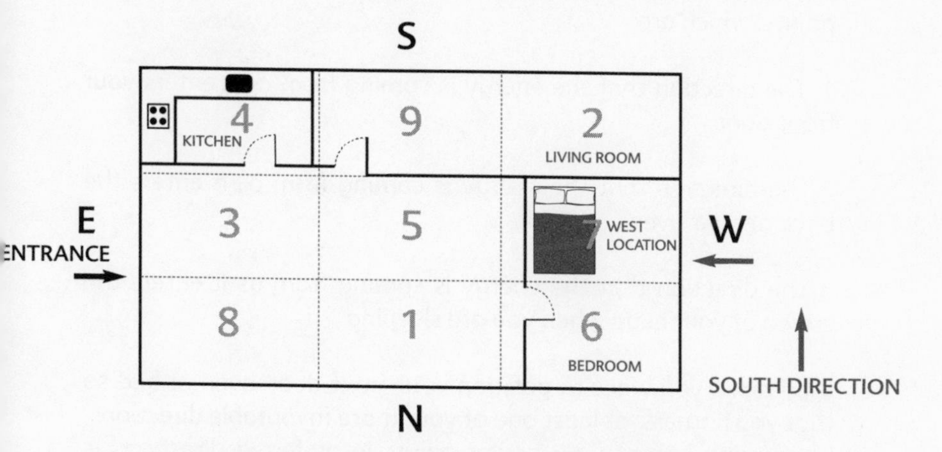

Here the location the two people are sleeping in is in the West, the direction they are sleeping is towards the south. The main door is facing east, the oven is also facing east.

You want to harness your preferred directions at the three power points, which are:

1. The direction that the energy is coming from as it enters your front door.

2.The direction that the energy is coming from as it enters the back of your oven.

3.The direction that the energy is coming from as it enters the crown of your head when you are sleeping.

If possible, you want to position your front door, oven or bed so that you harness at least one of your more favourable directions. Harnessing one of your power points in preferred directions is good . . . harnessing two is great . . . harnessing all three would be excellent.

If it isn't possible to harness any of your preferred directions, there are solutions via colour, symbols, element etc. (see page 142).

In a partnership situation, if you need differing directions, compromise is the solution. The female chooses her better sleeping position, the male his better door location. Vice versa if the female is the bigger breadwinner.

In ascertaining your best directions it is not that the last four directions are 'bad' for you, they simply enhance to a lesser degree, for example:

- A nap in the afternoon is good for you . . . not having one isn't bad for you.
- A glass of water with fresh lemon as vitamin C is good for you . . . not having one isn't bad for you.

To illustrate this point further, I'll use a sleeping example.

Let's take 'A' as your comfortable norm and at 'A' you get five hours sleep and you're OK on that.
At 'B' you may get five hours, ten minutes. If you had that extra ten minutes you would feel even better — this is equivalent to the support of your 7th direction.
At 'C' you may get five hours, twenty minutes, and feel even better still — equivalent to your 6th direction. At 'D' etc . . .

It's not that your 6th, 7th or 8th directions are bad for you, it's that the first four are even more beneficial!

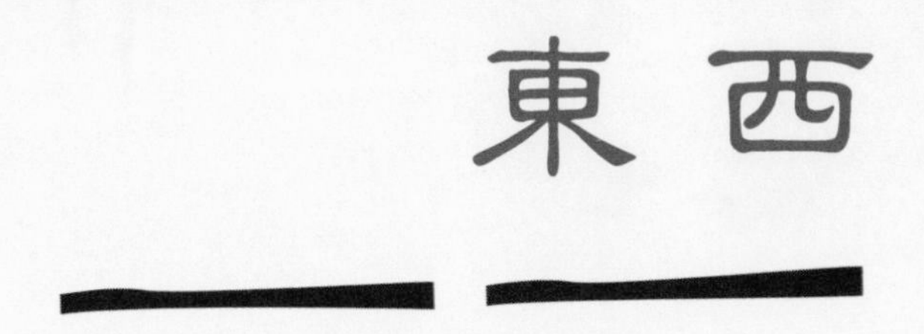

So is that it?
Will my life be perfect now?

Before you get carried away and run off to buy those mirrors and fountains, Feng Shui is not some kind of panacea. Life is about creating inner — outer balance. If you have internal psychological blockages, and are using Feng Shui to fix your outer house in the hope that it will fix your inner house and achieve happiness and fulfilment, that may be a bit wishful. The enhancements could attract your desires but you may sabotage them. Sometimes it is just the environment that needs attention and that's great, but if internally you have a message running saying something like; 'I don't deserve . . .' or 'Things never work out for me . . .', 'I'll never be a success . . .', you need to eradicate your saboteur. Feng Shui principles at the least will give you visually pleasing design but you can't really get on the outside what you're not ready to receive on the inside (see page 156). Sorry to mention it, but this is good old quantum theory again . . . you affect the results and visa versa. Inner — outer . . . Yin — Yang.

What you expect is mostly what you get.

Feng Shui – Life's harmony via environmental analysis.
What do you think?

Is this oriental hokus pokus . . . ?

I think not. It is a gift cloaked in mystery and when that cloak is removed it reveals a profound design tool.

Einstein gave us quantum physics – this is simply its harbinger, quantum design.

春山牧歌

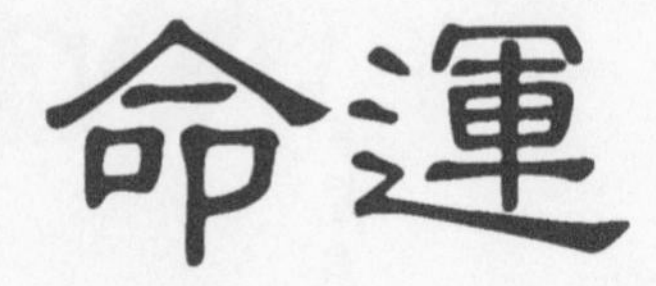

As the Beach boys sang all those years ago

I wish you

GOOD
GOOD
GOOD

GOOD VIBRATIONS

UNVEILING THE MYTHS
and rumours

SO WHAT IS ALL THIS ABOUT SUPERSTITIONS, GOOD LUCK, BAD LUCK, TOILETS, MIRRORS, FISH, and so on . . .

There is a great deal of myth and rumour perpetuated by some enthusiasts of Feng Shui. I would like to take this opportunity to share some of my experiences in the field and in so doing clear up some of the ambiguity surrounding a few of those stories. I have chosen the ones that I believe most people are curious about. This is, of course, a personal perspective and though a relatively informed one, you will no doubt ask your own questions and discern for yourself.

思想

Toilets!!

Many of you will have heard or read the tale about toilets and their supposed bad energy, to such a degree that you probably believe in order to harness the benefits of Feng Shui the only sensible thing to do seems to be to get rid of them, and just use one at a friendly neighbour's house.

You can probably guess by my tone that I am about to dismiss the myth. Sorry, I know it has probably generated a lot of good jokes but . . . toilets!

I have clients who have panicked because they read in a book that they mustn't have their toilet in the southeast (represents wealth and blessings) or their wealth will flush away. They mustn't have their toilet in the west or they will have no joy in their life — and definitely not in the southwest — their relationship corner!

No wonder some people don't want to bother with Feng Shui. Can you imagine not being able to have a toilet in your office or home?

選擇

So what is the answer?

In ancient times there were no toilets in the city of Peking, its noble inhabitants used pots carried in to the fields and emptied by servants.

and no – this is not the answer!

In the 21st century we are not dealing with the kind of sanitation they had thousands of years ago. Back then they may have used superstitions to ensure that local populations would protect themselves in the area of hygiene, and so prevent the manifestation of negative energy.

In China, running water is mostly considered auspicious, so why would running water in a toilet be bad luck? The fear may have been that the toilet in syphoning water away was syphoning abundance away, but actually it is continually expelling negative Chi and pulling in fresh water. It is not leaking the water and so wasting it, it is always under your control, unless of course it is broken. Waterfalls and toilets are both about water recycling, in fact the toilet gets rid of waste and replenishes itself with fresh water. That sounds pretty good to me.

The notion that a toilet in the wealth area is flushing away money is fable, supported by our negative psychological association towards this area of our environments. Psychologically most people tend to view toilets as unclean and this stigma has fuelled support for the folklore.

In the last century we made giant leaps forward in the health and hygiene of our environments. In fact in their fastidious attempt to clean what is seen as unclean, some people's bathrooms are cleaner than their kitchens.

Treat your toilet areas and bathrooms as appreciated rooms in your building and respect them for the ease and comfort they offer that people didn't have back then.

Energetically, the toilet is considered an open channel to the sewers of your town or city, so put the lid down. Even books on etiquette suggest this. Symbolically, the idea is to close off the awareness of waste. Attempt to keep the bathroom door closed — a spring will do this. It is suggested that something reflective be placed on the outside of the door. Ideally, endeavour to change your attitude to toilets; in so doing you will change the energy you project onto this area. The energy you give, is what you get back. A less than positive perspective towards this zone could subdue the energy returned. Transform it into a place you actually 'like'.

Negative projections apply to anything you don't like. If its an object you don't like and don't need, give it away.

Projecting a negative attitude creates negative Chi. This is why when you are in the company of people you don't like, or that don't like you — you wither — literally.

How you think and feel, is how it is.

Make your choice — discern.

OBJECTS — SPACES — PEOPLE

Mirrors

Mirrors in the bedroom or not?

Although mirrors are not referred to in the
old texts, a mirror does reflect you and your whole energy field. Some cultures believe that a mirror traps the soul, and many believe that this is why in Feng Shui we don't have mirrors reflecting our bodies when we sleep, so as to allow the soul to journey at night. This is a mystical view! A practical perspective is that in reflecting in a mirror we are literally bouncing our energy back at ourselves. Interacting with the refracting light so to speak, creating a dynamic energy flow, an expansion of vibration resulting in a shallower sleep. When we sleep we don't want to encourage a dynamic flow of energy, we want to rest, we want peace. So if you want deeper sleep, I would suggest that you don't have a mirror reflecting your body.

Money plants ... mmmmm!

With its name alone, therein lies power.

Of course, putting them in the wealth area of the southeast whose element is wood is rather symbiotic. That these plants are also hardy and succulent adds a strong healthy image.

The money plant has garnered some of its notoriety and popularity for many reasons. The association of its name, combined with it representing the wood element contributes to this. Most plants placed in the southeast are beneficial.

'Beams'

What is the story behind exposed beams and their supposed health problems . . . ?

Here my understanding of the esoteric meets my building experience, and again that good old quantum theory. We've established that everything is a vibration. As elements are a composite of particles, the steel or timber beams, as elements, are composed of these vibrating particles. Generally a beam spans between pressure points that bear the vertical and horizontal weight of a floor or roof and walls above. Supporting such pressure creates a tension in the beam itself. Engineers understand this and apply such knowledge when calculating the size and ratio of supporting structures needed to tolerate specific stress loads on building sites. The pressure of the weight bearing down generally from above creates a tension in the particles of the beam, this triggers an expression of that vibrational tension below the beam itself.
As ripples in a pond ultimately flow to the shore, so this pressure field travels too, until it reaches a denser surface. This is the field of pressure I refer to when suggesting that we avoid working or sleeping under a beam if possible. The degree to which it may affect you depends on your degree of sensitivity to that ripple's pressure and your tolerance of it.

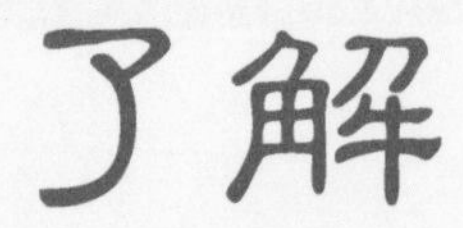

A network of beams spreading the load is preferred if you must sit or lie beneath them for an extended time. (an area where you sit infrequently isn't a problem) A good idea is to round off their horizontal edges so as to avoid eddies of cutting Chi. If you are willing, fixing a false ceiling underneath dissipates some of this pressure field. Casing each beam individually is less effective and still creates cutting Chi.

Feng Shui is not intending to dictate a proliferation of 'zen' environments, its application simply liberates you to have a broader choice based on a relatively still environmental foundation. It endeavours to achieve a gentle flow of energy through balance. That way your final choice of visual design and décor can display personal taste – vibrant or gentle. Without initial stillness there isn't really a choice.

A rather 'fishy' story

Goldfish in an aquarium in your southeast wealth area? The problem with goldfish is they die – what association would that have for you in your wealth area?

If you do choose to have fish in an aquarium or pond, then how many?

I have heard from many masters that nine fish in the southeast are auspicious, especially if there is a black one that can be the martyr, so to speak, the one that absorbs the negative energy. Some of us have this unfortunate role in life, it's called being a scapegoat, again illustrating the Chinese understanding that how we live and work with our environment is a reflection of our inner world.

One of the nine fish being black leaves eight 'gold'fish. Gold represents wealth and the number eight is most auspicious in China – symbolising abundance. Confusion sets in when some say seven fish, five fish and others, three fish, sometimes all in the same book. The Chinese seem to prefer an odd number believing this averts evil. It is also rumoured that the different numbers of fish can signify sexual vigour, abundance, and creativity.

OK would someone please stand up and give the definitive number. I'm beginning to feel a bit odd, like a fish out of water . . . is it three, five, seven or nine?

Teasing apart, what I can assuredly say is that in China, as in many cultures, water is considered auspicious. Philosophically the Chinese attitude is that water offers itself as nourishment and asks for nothing in return.

As a symbol, fish represent success in China, one of the reasons being that their movement in a pond stimulates Chi, aerating otherwise stagnant water. The movement of water is one of the reasons water fountains are popular, in addition, the water's spray creates negative ions, which are uplifting mood alterers.

Healthy fish in a clean aerated aquarium or pond are a powerful image: the visually stimulating beauty of them swimming with ease in the rippling water is a positive stimulus that enhances the Chi of the observer as well as that of the location. Back to the old Heisenberg Principle – observed affecting the observer. This is, of course, unless your senses are offended by seeing fish confined. Only you will know its personal impact as a symbol affecting your subconscious; what it means to you is its inherent power.

心靈

Superstition and symbolism

Symbolic images and superstitions are separated by a very fine line. Symbolism has a somewhat logical base to it, superstition does not. That is unless you know its full story and can discern the message.

The image of the 1970s 'smile' motif is symbolic of 'happy' and is pretty obvious across all cultures. This is not superstition, it has a symbolism that says smile.

A popular folklore character in China mentioned in some of the books, and one I am often asked about, is the three-legged frog as a symbol for wealth and success. Unless a three-legged frog means wealth and success to you at a deep level I suggest you use a more culturally familiar Western image. Then you are really accessing the psychology of design that Feng Shui can harness. Sometimes these abstracted oriental images of frogs, lions, dragons etc. become charms or talisman that can erroneously tap into people's religious leanings, through superstitions that aren't culturally relevant. Obviously one must nurture one's personal beliefs, but charms and talismen are misplaced in any assumed association with the original Feng Shui, which, as I said, was based on an analysis of the way of the natural world and our interaction with it.

了解

I am attempting here to distil folklore from fact and yet I know I myself began by referring to a legend, that of the turtle. It is the ancients ensuing observation and analysis of the environment on which Feng Shui has been based, not the tale of the turtle. Feng Shui is a kind of philosophy of environmental alchemy inclusive of the human element. So although it enters into the realm beyond current conscious knowing, it is based on hundreds, nay thousands, of years of observation and research, not a tale told of one person's experience manifested into lore.

With the three-legged frog and its associated image of luck, folklore characters and fables do have power as all placebos do – the power we give them. We have our own superstitions and beliefs in the West and are culturally able to recognise them as such and to differentiate. If the frog works for you, great, but other more personally meaningful images could potentially offer more constructive power, working at both a conscious and unconscious level. If you want to use the three-legged frog, find out the myth and its meaning.

I don't personally hate the old toad — but to me him being three-legged already seems rather unfortunate as opposed to fortunate. Some may declare, 'Oh but I placed a three-legged frog in my wealth area, and even though I didn't fully know its origins, the most wonderful things happened.' I am thrilled for them and I would ask them to consider that maybe they were ready internally and externally for those things to happen. The frog was a symbol for the power their minds and hearts had to create their desires, another object endowed with that strength of belief may have created a similar result. Of course, I can't say for sure, but I do know our homes and offices do not have to look like Chinese restaurants in order to harness the power of Feng Shui.

This is where that fine line between symbolism and superstition enters — both impact deeply on the psyche.

If an individual from Germany, post-1933, had suggested you place a swastika in your east sector for eternal life, you may well have considered him sick, up to sculduggery or at the least misguided. The swastika was in fact the Chinese symbol for eternal life but when used in Germany it was drawn in the reverse, i.e. back to front. Whether Mr H reversed it in error or intent we cannot know, but his insignia grew to represent quite the opposite of eternal life. If Mr H reversing the symbol of eternal life was a conscious decision, then the resulting destruction was truly symbolic.

Symbolic images affect us and our psyche, setting up subconscious messages. Image has power, that is why we use pictorial images as symbols to convey a shorthand message. Advertising executives know this and they apply its subliminal principles to many successful campaigns.

In the smaller picture, literally — that one opposite your desk in the office, maybe a meaningless image bought in a poster shop, perhaps a cartoon of someone tripping over himself — it is humorous and hypnotic. Every time you look up, it is symbolically impacting on your psyche for you to trip up. I use this to illustrate the power of symbolism presented in a cultural reference we can understand, knowing this, it would be better to put up an image that inspires you, one that illustrates where you want to go and how you want to be. However healthy and vital you are, if your environment is projecting negative messages it will suppress your potential. It's not that you shouldn't have witty and humorous images on your walls, just that you need to be more conscious about how and where you place them.

哲學

IMAGES AND THEIR INHERENT SYMBOLISM ARE VERY POWERFUL. APART FROM THEIR SIMPLISTIC AND OFTEN OBVIOUS MEANING, THERE IS A WHOLE OTHER LEVEL THAT SUBLIMINALLY IMPACTS ON THE ARCHETYPES OF OUR PSYCHOLOGICAL MAP AND TOO OFTEN THIS IS IGNORED IN DESIGN WHEN IT COULD OFFER SUPPORT.

So what's all this about GOOD LUCK and BAD LUCK?

One of my clients, as a result of advice prior to my coming to consult, had viewed the south (place of reputation) as bad luck because it was her seventh preferred direction. Fearing it was bad for her, she left it barren, devoid of any potential negativity, as she saw it. Her logic was that if she improved it, she was improving a zone that was bad for her and so increasing its potential to affect her adversely. To add to the dismal way she was increasingly feeling, she had used a lot of navy in the décor to represent water, a colour she was advised to use for this reason, but which she found depressing. She was hoping to exhaust the fire energy of the south i.e. with water (navy) putting out the fire of the south. Similarly she had stripped the southeast. The result: she was sad, she saw no light in her future and feared for her finances.

Feng Shui is about balance. You do not strip half your home away. I was most concerned to see this client so trustingly demolished into fear. This case and many others like it triggered a need in me to comment in this book.

Like many of us to varying degrees, this client was innocently looking for a quick fix. She was desperate to change her situation, but what you focus on is where you put your God-given energy. Instead of being able to focus on the positive orientations to actively benefit her life, all she could think about was the damage the southeast and south areas might be creating.

This misunderstanding resulted from an erroneous view of the information that the Chinese believe the different areas of the magnetic forcefield have different life-specific qualities, which serve each of us in different ways. Because you have directions that support you more, it doesn't mean the others are bad luck. Your preferred order of directions is listed in descending order of support. That is they SUPPORT you in descending order. The last four do not cause loss, serious illness or death as proposed in some scarily popular books on Feng Shui (see page 67). This is a more recent and superstitious addition laid on top of the original analysis, generally by superstitious consultants who either believe in the legends, or are too impressionable themselves to question their own masters. The definition of superstition is: misdirected reverence or irrational fear of the unknown. Superstitions tend to offer a warning, with a tendency to being fear-based – even when suggesting good luck, i.e. if you do 'X' it's good luck but if you don't do 'X' does that mean it's bad luck?

I am simply trying to express a concern here, because it is often not the tale that holds the power but our belief in the tale. Superstitions have power; mind over matter. Apply them if you wish but remember they are not the foundation of Feng Shui. The core of Feng Shui is based on element analysis, form and the energy meridians of the planet.

It was not set up within the magnificent genius of creation that the sun of the south or the joy of the west would bring bad luck to some. No: all the orientations serve us. 'Serve' being the operative word, i.e. benefit us. Some more so than others but none of them are negative. The universe is gloriously more complex and loving than that. Enhance all the areas of your environment. Treat each of them as if they were areas of your heart. You would not willingly leave out a part of that – I hope!

It has been suggested to me by historians that some of this mis-information may have been propagated a few hundred years ago by the ruling powers at that time, in order to stimulate a sense of fear in the local populace and so create a passive suppression. I do not know if this is so, but I do know that these tales have created grief and havoc for some of my more suggestible clients and even for some of those who are more resilient but whom having recognised the power of Feng Shui principles in many other ways, have assumed that the expert or master has this information on some kind of esoteric authority.

There are many stories of people making major structural changes to satisfy the advice of a consultant, sometimes effectively, sometimes not. Remember this territory is about balance, and as in many fields experts have limitations – their own personal ones, which they, like you and me, bring with them into their working skill. If the change seems and feels good to you, that is the initial litmus test. If it doesn't feel right, listen to your instincts, our own mistakes are far more palatable than someone else's.

選擇

Discernment

Similarly, another of my clients was in great distress because he had been told that unless he moved his child out of a particular location and orientation his child would become very sick indeed.

Excuse me! Did God enter the room?

I beg you to discern. If anyone suggests severe sickness and death will result from a particular orientation of the magnetic forcefield, tell them to take their superstitious negative chatter back to the supposed master who taught it! It is fear-based teaching. Fear is not a place of wisdom, and ignorance by its nature does not recognise itself.

The workings of our universe have a genius to them. It was not set up so that a child of a particular gender, born in a particular year, would be sick or die if they lay in or faced a certain direction.

That would be like suggesting that we can only live in the equivalent of half the magnetic forcefield. It would be like the proverbial joke of trying to dig half a hole – RIDICULOUS.

Feng Shui is a powerful tool but the superstitions placed on it are just that — superstitions. And if we believe we are vulnerable to them, that belief creates its own resulting grief.

The Chinese culture is strongly based in folklore so a tradition has built up over recent time of using the characters from parables as cures to ward off bad luck and attract good luck. Lots of the original tales they are based on have been forgotten or enhanced, and the resulting fable has become a kind of ritual, which has become its own kind of lore. It's one of the reasons I called my first book *Chinese Whispers*, I chose as best I could to go back to the original whisper.

Note:
In issues surrounding current environmental health concerns, references to damage caused by power cables, generating stations and the territory of geopathic stress, where there is a disturbance in the earth's crust, are quite separate to advice given in the above situations (see page 152).

了解

It used to be thought that left-handed people were unlucky and now they are perceived as gifted.

It was said that people with prominent foreheads had a more primitive perspective on life, now it is proposed they have greater scholarly potential.

I am suggesting that we avoid being at the mercy of humanity's limitations. The best we can do is get more conscious and hone our discernment. Otherwise we are going to be limited by experts' limitations, my own included.

Despite all this . . . PLEASE resist the temptation of throwing the proverbial baby out with the bath water just because some less-aware individuals have placed superstitions on top of the original genius and then forgotten that it was not part of the original.

Return to its origins – Feng Shui is a wonderful source of information for creating balance and harmony in an environment.

陰

古

14th-century speaker:

'White light is a collection of all the other colours of the spectrum.'

14th-century man:

'Don't be silly . . . colour comes from plants and pigments in the ground and white is the absence of colour.'

15th-century speaker:

'White light is a collection of all the other colours of the spectrum.'

15th-Century man:

'Oh, I know that, every one knows that.'

20th-century speaker:

'Feng Shui evolved in China over 4,000 yrs ago as a simple device to create integrated life-enhancing environments.'

20th-century man:

'Oh that's just nonsense and superstition.'

22nd-century speaker:

'Feng Shui evolved in China over 4,000 yrs ago as a simple device to create integrated life-enhancing environments, used in building site surveys all around the world.'

22nd-century man:

'Oh, I know that.'

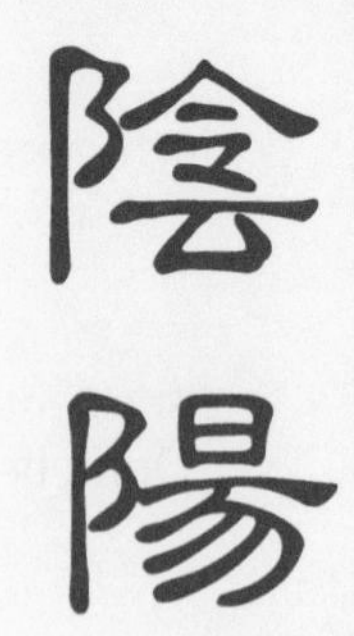

I wish you a smile in your heart.

廣重画
保永堂
僊鶴堂

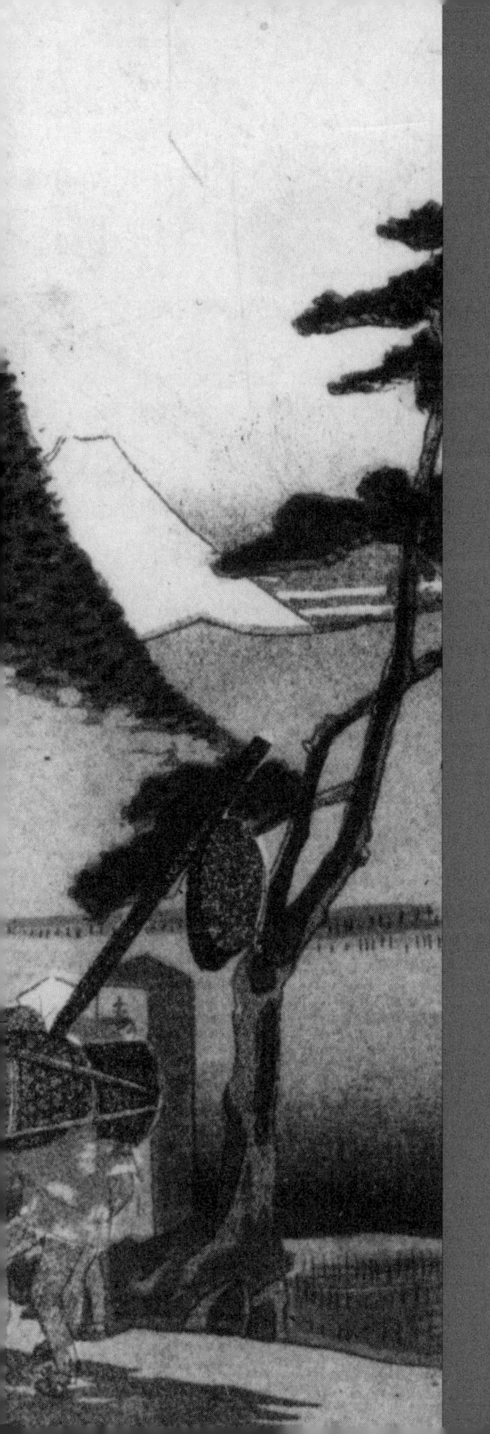

ADVICE AND TIPS

HOW TO APPLY THIS INFORMATION IN OUR DAILY REALITY

It can be hard to create a perfect environment but since we now know that everything is vibration this might explain better why we feel good in one building yet not another.

The ancient sages propose that this is our Chi interacting with the Chi of the environment.

Chi, in simplistic terms, is the flow of the vibration as an invisible forcefield radiating from everything: objects, materials, structures of all shapes and sizes and much more, including ourselves, creating harmony or discord.

So with this awareness here are some simple guidelines and tips that can help improve your home and office towards an ideal.

These tips may seem rather simplistic – but they need to be for easy understanding and application. Life is, after all, a complex composite of simple parts; if we balance the simple we harmonise the complex whole.

This first section is a short easy 'must do' list followed by a more detailed one for those who have the time and the inclination.

QUICK-FIX LIST

Like that old adage that says you never get a second chance at a first impression, at an esoteric level your entrance is a gateway . . . inviting positive energy into you environment.

Think about the impression you need or wish to give. Imagine yourself as a visitor, what impression would your entrance have on you? At all levels be conscious. If this is an office, is your name displayed in clear print? And does your company's logo reflect a positive projection?

Is your entrance welcoming, is it easy to enter, or difficult to approach? Does it say push when the mechanism needs to be pulled, with visitors left feeling exasperated or even feeling foolish before they meet you?

A cheery uplifting sign as you exit your home or office can be a nice touch. What you see as you leave your environment affects your approach to the outside world.

If your door has a double or triple digit number place the first number at eye level (around five feet) and then place each consecutive number a little higher than the previous one.

Is there an ease of flow around your furniture, for movement of self and Chi?

Clear your space so it's clutter free-ish.

Use comfortable seating preferably with its backs to the wall. If your back is to the door, and you have no choice, no problem: just position a mirror or something reflective, so you can see the door. This is less critical in your own safe home.

Put peaceful images where you choose to have more restful energy.

Feng Shui is not about designing meditative Zen dens, it's about creating spaces that reflect your needs and dreams. You want to be surrounded by images and points of focus that you love, which inspire feelings of joy, peace and/or are aspirational. If there are images and objects you hate, find a friend or colleague who loves them or just sell them/give them away.

Images and symbols have power: we associate red with danger – a green stop sign would be most disconcerting! What messages are impacting on you from your environment? That picture of a weeping child, check out whether its beauty lifts your spirits or depresses you. Single images in your relationship sector encourage the potential for more singleness in your life – maybe you want that – maybe you don't.

Remember to use colours that enhance your Kua number.

Add healthy plants especially near computers and TVs to absorb electromagnetic discharge. Preferably use soft, round-leaved ones, unless your joy of cacti is compromised.

Use full-spectrum lighting so that all the eye cones are engaged. Avoid fluorescents if you can, as they have a subtle flicker that is headache and fatigue-inducing.

Remember to repeatedly empty those rubbish bins.

If there isn't running water (such as a small fountain) or an ioniser in the room then simply use a water spray once or twice a day to ionise the air. Washing down your desk with water each day can be a simple and effective way, and if you can, do this in the home too.

Use natural scents or enhanced organic ones and keep the place clean.

If it's broken . . . fix it, if it isn't, don't.

This is about your life integrating as a whole, it is not about Feng Shui becoming your driving force. Feng Shui is simply a support along life's way, so let it help you and enjoy getting into the flow.

和諧

Before we go into the more detailed section, here is some general advice about the one you've heard a great deal about in the popular press . . . CLUTTER.

I know it sounds rather pedestrian but it's pretty logical that where there is chaos energy doesn't flow with ease.

Since our outer world reflects our inner world it just may be worth the effort of clearing it. Clutter can come in all sorts of guises, the obvious 'stuff' that you are going to clear the moment you get a chance, but that chance seems to procrastinate itself right out of your diary. Decluttering is not about throwing things away just for the sake of it, obviously you will make your own considerations, but if it has been there and unused for two years or more . . . well what do you think?

That pile stacked on top of the children's wardrobe, not only do the children not use it because they can't reach it, but positioned there so high up it creates a sense of pressure in their little lives, especially when they wake up and see it first thing in the morning. And if it's above your own wardrobe . . . ditto!

身體

This isn't about being obsessively tidy, it's about removing the excess that may be deterring you from where you want to go in life. Often we hold on to something to respect the memory and value it had for us at one time, or in case we need it one day. We become quite attached to the clutter in our life, even broken items. Stuffed in cupboards, stuffed on to shelves, hidden under the bed. Maybe it served you once, now it doesn't . . . thank it, clear it and enjoy the new potential the cleared space creates. I have often heard the refrain: 'Oh, but just when I let go of things I find I need them'. That may be because the energetic clear-out has triggered a resurge of energy to use it, when prior to its exit it may have sat there for another five years. Hanging on to unused objects in case you need them one day sends out an internal message of lack – a message that says when you do need it you won't be able to afford a replacement. Let go, trust yourself and your ability to satisfy your needs.

Identify your need to hold on to STUFF, and notice where in your environment that may be. Is it by the front door? Clutter by your front door blocks your approach to the world, especially if it faces south. Just look where the clutter is in your office or home. Clutter in the west and it will be more difficult to get projects off the ground. It would be interesting to see if the clutter is in the relationship sector and whether relationships in the office are difficult or there is difficulty in emotional relationships at home.

Sometimes clutter is created as a subconscious obstacle, blocking your potential success. Energy needs to be free to flow without obstruction for your life to reflect that. Check out where you have clutter and ask yourself if you want to potentially block this area of your life.

If you have an object you don't like but which was given to you by a good friend, give it to someone who does like it, your appreciation is for the gesture, the gift was given with affection and hopefully received in that way, that is the real exchange — let it go. As best you can, file and dispose of papers, create a space that respects you and your needs. Just clearing the clutter so it isn't on your mind as something you must do is such a plus in itself. I know it all sounds like a lot of common sense when we read about it, yet often until we read about it and its effects, we don't get round to clearing it.

Everything is vibration — REMEMBER — endeavour to invite life-enhancing vibrations. Clutter isn't one of them and it affects you mentally, physicaly and emotionally.

I SUPPOSE THAT SINCE THE CHINESE BELIEVE THERE IS A NATURAL ORDER TO CREATION, WHETHER WE APPLY FENG SHUI PRINCIPLES IMMEDIATELY OR NEXT MONTH IS ALL PERFECTLY IN ITS TIMELY PLACE . . .
JUST LIKE YOUR CLUTTER WAS UNTIL NOW.

辦公室

THE OFFICE

Feng Shui is not about creating laid back zen-type environments – in calculating the needs of an office it may be to create a very active dynamic.

Avoid thresholds and doormats bearing your company's logo, you don't want people walking all over you.

Some images generate a positive feeling and are inspirational, others the reverse. Negative images deplete our energy. What message does your office project and is that what you want, including your business's signboard, logo and even its business cards?

Water represents money to the Chinese so images of water pouring in, such as a waterfall are considered very auspicious especially in one's southeast sector.

Allow as much sunlight and fresh air as possible to enter your environment.

If your windows do not open, and you have several computers and copiers which are generating electro-magnetic charges, introduce some plants. These absorb the negative Chi whilst simultaneously emanating positive Chi.

Excess positive ions in the air created by the electronic machinery encourage fatigue. As mentioned earlier, one way to increase negative ions in the air is to wash the surface of your desk daily with water, or to use an ionizer or a simple water spray.

Your desk and work area are a reflection of your mental state and vice versa, so clear it as best you can.

The location of your office or desk is extremely important to harness good Chi.

There should be easy access to your desk.

If you cannot see the door and you can't move your desk, strategically place a mirror or reflective surface.

Curved desks are best for creativity but too many curves in the office and you may not manage your money too well.

If there are two people in a room. one with their back to the window and one with their back to the wall, the one with their back to the wall will feel more secure and so be in a more powerful position.

If a toilet door is visible from your desk camouflage it with a picture, a mirror or something similar.

Obviously if you work from home, apply whatever is appropriate from the above and have fresh flowers on the desk to stimulate the Chi.

Place a bright reading-lamp on your desk, to inspire a bright future (south – fame, reputation).

Put your telephone on the left if you are right-handed, the reverse for left-handed people, so you don't literally get crossed wires when you are conversing and attending to notes simultaneously.

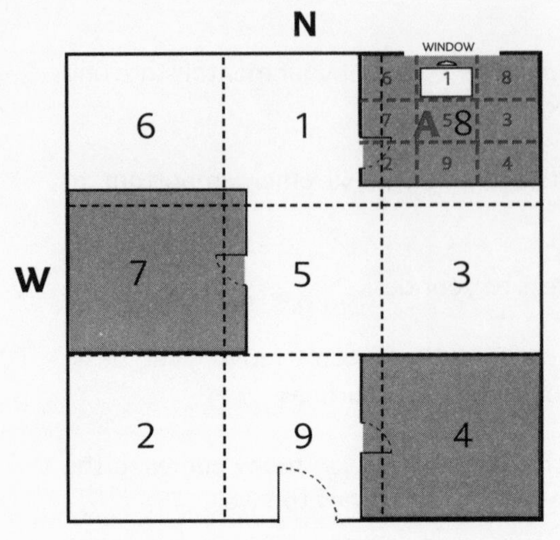

OFFICE A
Here the occupant's birth date is 10 April 1956. So his Kua number is 8.

Sitting north within his inividual office is not his most supportive. Facing towards the south is not the most supportive.

With the window behind him, he is working in his own shadow,

In terms of the whole main office grid he is sitting in location 8 (northeast). This location is good for him although he could reposition himself diagonally to face 2 (southwest), his best direction, which would help compensate the other limitations mentioned above and place him within the northeast of his individual office. Earth colours would further support him.

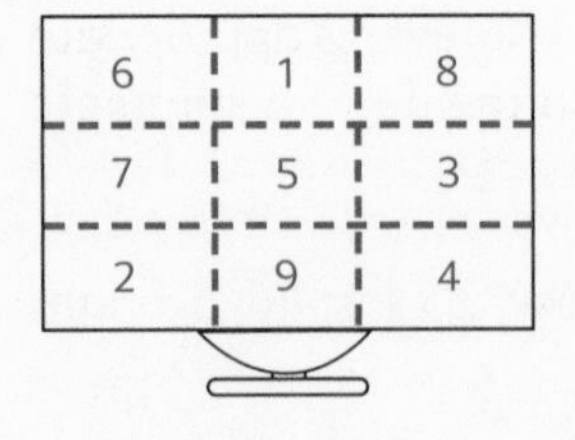

The same grid can be applied to a desk.

OFFICE B: Layout (i)

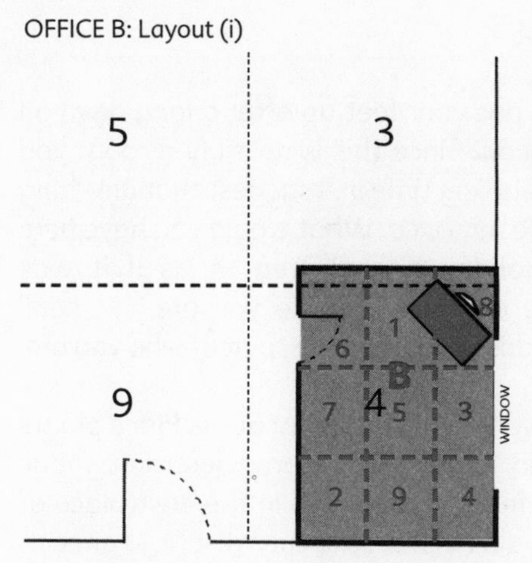

In this office, the accupant's date of birth is 5 June 1971, so his Kua number is 2.
So the northeast location (8) within the individual office supports him.
His back is to a solid corner and he can see the door.
The west energy coming through the door supports him as his second best direction and he is facing southwest at his desk, his fourth best direction.

In terms of the whole office he is sitting in location 4 (southeast). This location is not one of his best so he could bring in the elements and colours earth and fire for support.

OFFICE B: Layout (ii)

Here in layout B, however, the occupant's date of birth is 10 September 1953.
Her Kua number is 4.
She can also see the door but having her back to the window, she could feel vulnerable. Energy coming into the room is west energy. which is not the most support for her. The south (9) energy coming into the main office compensates. In terms of the whole main office, the area she is sitting in location 4 (southeast), which is good.

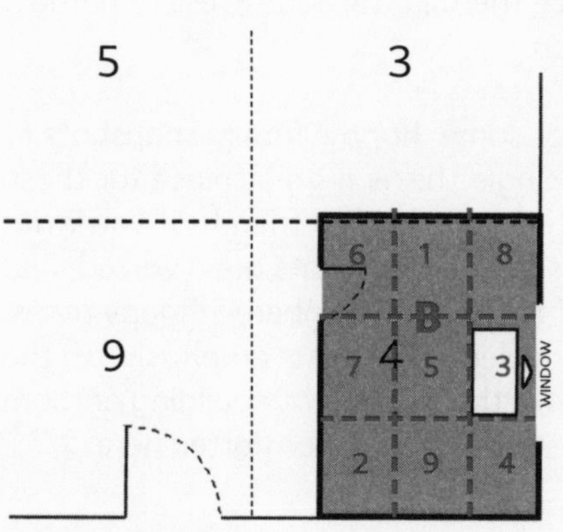

STUDY / DRAWING ROOM

When you come home and put your feet up after a long day you want this room to nourish you. Since this is possibly a room you spend a great deal of your relaxing time in, I suggest that anything you don't really like should be removed. What would you have here if this was your luxury holiday home? Treat it as if it was special, make it out of the ordinary just like you are . . . spoil yourself. Reward yourself — this is home to the spirit of who you are.

If there is a desk, place flowers on its south location. Place plants close to the television and stereo to absorb electromagnetic pollution. Music should preferably be placed in the east(place of thunder). The television should be placed in the west (joy) or east.

Position seating so that backs are to the walls if possible, if some seating has its back to the door position a reflective surface so you can see the door.

This is often the room where those wedding or celebration pictures are on show, so place them in the southwest to harness the benefit of prolonged union.

In the west of this room place some 'happy' family snapshots of everyone together. If you're single this is a great place for those images remembering great times with good friends. If you want to put up family photographs but your parents are divorced, find individual pictures of each of them at remembered happy times. If family members are deceased place the emphasis of the memorabilia relating to them in the east of your building or room (place of ancestors). Their resting energy is comforted here.

THE DINING ROOM

Place shy guests in the position where they can see the door – they will feel more confident.
Yellow is a gathering colour – so its very good for social locations.
Mirrors are very good in the dining room as they double the nourishment.
Round tables represent heaven's blessings.

KITCHEN

The kitchen is considered one of the more important rooms because it is where the food is prepared. Food represents inner wealth and well being.

If the first thing you see on entering the property is the kitchen door, you may nibble more frequently. Set up some kind of screen or place a mirror on the kitchen door so that it is concealed in a decorative way.

Fire and water should not be placed next to each other. A wooden chopping board or small plant on the counter between them mitigates the conflict. A painting or photograph of plants would work as a symbolic alternative.

THE MAIN BEDROOM

The balance of this room affects the whole household and is especially appropriate for relationship enhancements. Have images of union and pairs of items here – perhaps two rose quartz crystals, which represent heart energy, placed in the southwest.

Avoid sleeping under a structural beam, if it runs parallel and central to the bed it can disturb your sleep and may encourage a sense of separation from your partner. This is due to the field of pressure it generates. If you can't avoid this then create a canopy over the bed to act as a shield and use uplighters at your bedside. Similarly, beams running horizontally can create discomfort.

Preferably have a solid wall behind the bed. When lying in bed, avoid having your feet pointing directly to the door. If you have no choice, put some kind of barrier such as a cabinet or chest at the foot of the bed. It is preferable not to have your head directed towards the door wall. Again if there is no choice, position a mirror so that you can see the door from the bed. Your inherent caveman instincts want you to be safe at night.

Don't put fresh flowers in a bedroom as these are energising and therefore do not aid sleep.

Activate the corner that relates to career success (north) by placing a bright light there or a painting/image of a beautiful flowing water scene . . . not a storm though, you don't need emotional conflict in your work.

CHILDREN' S BEDROOMS

The west location is good as it represents joy, creativity and the resting energy of sunset. If you want more invigorating energy for the child, then place his or her bedroom in the east, the energy of the rising sun.

Don't put aggressive images in this room as they can have a subconscious impact.

Apply colours appropriate to the child's Kua number.

Children often turn in their beds as they sleep to orientate naturally to one of their preferred directions. Unknowingly, we adults turn them back — let nature choose.

BATHROOM

Check that toilets and sinks are in good working order (this includes sinks anywhere else). If they leak, it suggests waste. Attend to any blockages and keep plugs in bath and sink wastes.

Treat your bathroom as a room you wish to enjoy — indulge it as you would any other room. Keep the door closed — a spring can be used for this. The toilet is considered a channel to the sewers of your city, so keep the lid down.

Place a small convex mirror or something reflective on the outside of the door to deflect good energy from going into what you may still perceive as a negative zone.

THE GARDEN

A neglected overgrown garden is the external equivalent of internal clutter. Taking care of your garden is like taking care of yourself.

Place the grid onto your garden plot as you would onto your building. Here it is similarly based on the principle of balancing the opposing Yin and Yang – finding and working with its symbolism and colour etc.

Tall trees are Yang . . . horizontal foliage is Yin.
Light is Yang . . . shade is Yin.
Red flowers are Yang . . . violet flowers are Yin.

Create curving paths here rather than straight ones, meandering paths represent water.
Rockeries in a pond represent harmony – the rocks as symbols of mountains – Yang – and the water is Yin.

As with interiors use the elements in their relative locations.
West – perhaps a metal wind chime – blue, white or yellow flowers – round shapes are good here.
In the northwest – a stone sculpture (earth element) – yellow and orange flowers – round shapes.
Southwest – a bird bath attracts Chi and represents earth – yellow, orange and red flowers – square shapes.

North – a good position for a water feature – blue flowers – wavy shapes.
Northeast – maybe a rockery with red and yellow flowering plants – square shapes.
East – the greenest part of your garden – plant tall trees – rectangular shapes.
Southeast – a waterfall represents money pouring in and stimulates Chi – rectangular shapes.
South – fir trees/pine trees and red flowers – triangular shapes.

Place wooden furniture in the east and southeast (or south) and metal furniture in the northwest, west and north.

If you have sculptures in the garden, check that their image is a friendly one rather than an aggressive one, ultimately this depends on personal taste, of course. In the orient they use fierce lions and the like for protection.
Evergreen hedges are preferred as these suggest longevity. Pine, willow and cypress trees are especially auspicious due to their hardiness.

As in the west, flowers in China carry their own meaning . . . jasmine represents communication and friendship and is Yin.
Peonies represent wealth and honour and are Yang.
Bamboo represents growth and is Yang.
Willow represents grace and is Yin.

COLOUR

Colour can raise or lower our spirits, increase or deplete our energy, creating a sense of concentration or distraction. Avoid what interior design dictates unless it feels good to YOU.

The colours listed below represent the full range of their colour group: i.e. Red embraces scarlet, fuchsia, pink etc. Yellow embraces mustard, lemon, honey tones etc.

Yellow is invigorating and stimulates mental energy so it is good for an office. Ideal in the southwest, northeast, northwest and west area of a building. It also has a gathering quality, so a room you use for entertaining would benefit from it.

Green represents longevity and peace. Good in the east, south east and south.

Blue (navy) is good for a business where communication is a priority and for financial trading situations.

Violet is good if tranquillity is required.

Purple is a fire element and the colour of the philosopher, good if used in the south and northeast.

White is good in the west, northwest and north.

Grey represents metal and is good in the west and northwest and north.

Black represents water and money.

Red, although representing happiness to the Chinese, it is the most highly charged wavelength in the visual spectrum and so must be used with care, as too much can create discomfort. It is good in the south, southwest and northeast.

Brown is good in the knowledge section – northeast – and the southwest.

Orange is good as a highlight in creative/social environments. It is good in the southwest and northeast.

Gold and silver represent the metal element and are good in the west and northwest. Gold is often used in China with red because it is believed this brings luck and wealth.

Use colours that enhance your Kua number and that of significant others sharing the environment.

The different orientations have different influences and benefits. For example, a door facing . . .

North supports business/career
Northeast is good for scholars
East enhances family and unity
Southeast brings wealth and prosperity
South attracts recognition
Southwest enhances relationships with loved ones
West supports creativity and children of the household
Northwest encourages travel and unexpected support from outsiders

The following are general locations good for particular rooms within your home:

North – relaxation room, bedroom, store areas, office
Northeast – study, playroom, storeroom, office
East – kitchen, office area, dining room, playroom, bedroom.
Southeast – dining room, kitchen, office area.
South – study, entertaining room.
Southwest – master bedroom, entertaining room
West – bedroom, dining room, entertaining room
Northwest – dining room, master bedroom, office area

DESIGNED FOR YOU

I am interrupting the list of tips here to remind you to be conscious of design choices that serve YOU.
Feng Shui differs from much of our design today in that it is not just about an environment looking good. It takes account of the human experience and harnesses a kind of feel-good factor by creating a nurturing environment. When we feel good we function better and behave better and differently.

With reference to design generally, a nice exercise to get clear about your own intuitive choices is:
Switch the phone off . . . turn down the lights . . . sit back in your favourite chair – if you don't have one . . . get one. Then quietly, with your eyes closed imagine your room of choice . . . what colours would the walls be, what kind of intensity of lighting would you want in your space? Would it be wall lights? Stand lamps? Overhead lighting? Notice the details as well as what your broader choices are. What colour? Texture – image – atmosphere – sound – smells? What adjectives would describe your space, what adjectives would describe how you feel in the space? What mood do you want to create? What message do you want the environment to give and what would your initial steps be to achieving this? Write them down and then see what your important 'others' want.

If you can't get clear about what you want – get clear about what you don't want. Then like in the relativity inherent in Yin – Yang, consider their opposites and let them guide you.

AND NOW BACK TO DETAILS.

USING MIRRORS

. . . as I said earlier these are not mentioned in the original texts but have become a popular item in our culture.

The mirrors we use to dress should reflect our full form. Ensure that they are hung at the correct height. If they are too high and you can't see your feet, you may feel ungrounded, if too low cutting off the top of your body, they may stimulate headaches.

It is fine to see a mirror from your bed, but you do not want to be able to see your body reflected in it when lying down. This reflection would cause an expansion of vibration resulting in a more shallow sleep state.

Mirrors can be used to transform 'negative space' by creating the illusion of a full rectangle or square in an L or U-shaped room, creating a greater sense of balance.

When using mirrors, take care to notice what they are reflecting. You want to double positive images, not negative ones.

Do not place a mirror directly opposite a front door – this will deflect the energy back out.

Avoid sitting with your back to a mirror as this will reveal your shadow side and you may feel, and so be, more vulnerable.

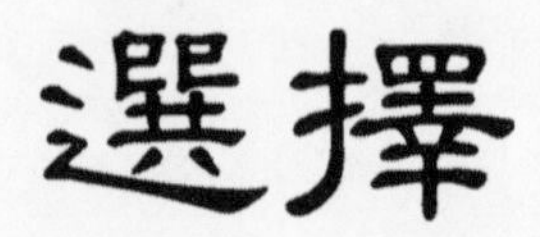

LIGHTING

Use full spectral lighting, which is similar to the quality of daylight, especially in offices, so that all the eye is engaged. Often the lighting we use is yellow in its illumination which only uses the middle area of the eye cones. This can cause you to tire more easily.

Poor lighting causes energy to stagnate.

If the room has a sloping roof, place an uplighter on the floor, this has the affect of pushing the energy upwards. Uplighters in a basement area literally raise the Chi.

Lights can be placed externally to create an illusionary square for an L-shaped building, this helps to compensate the negative space (see page 138).

If something in your life needs brightening up, literally place a, light or uplighter there e.g. southwest — love life, north — career.

Replace broken bulbs

PLANTS AND FLOWERS

Plants symbolise life and growth, and increase the oxygen in the environment.
Peace lillies, spider plants, Chinese evergreen, cheese plants are all hardy and recommended for their ease of care and beneficence.

Externally, cacti represent protection, internally they can feel threatening. Their spines create a sharper Chi in the immediate vicinity, beyond that the choice is personal, more Yang than Yin.

思想

WIND CHIMES

Wind chimes can be used internally and externally, their purpose is to moderate Chi not to activate it. They are good for defining different areas – the air current creates a sound-wave defining movement from one area to another (inaudible even – wind-chimes don't need to be heard to work – vibration stuff !).

If there are a number of doors in a row, place a wind chime above the central one to moderate the flow of chi.

Make sure that your wind chimes have hollow tubes and that for you their sound is harmonious.

Placing a wind chime at your front door can enhance the energy entering your building, especially helpful if its direction is not one of your most supportive ones.

Avoid hanging a wind chime above your bed or desk as the movement of Chi could disturb your sleep and/or concentration respectively.

If your staircase directly aligns with your front door, place a wind chime near the inside of your door to prevent the flow of Chi from rushing out. Additionally in this situation, place a reflective disc on the inside of your door to reflect the energy back into the building.

天體

CRYSTALS

Crystals can be used as enhancers in specific areas

There are two distinctly different categories of crystal, these are uncut mineral crystals such as amethyst etc. or clear, faceted lead crystals.

As the sunlight passes through the faceted lead crystal it refracts the light, splitting it into its full spectrum of colours. This splitting of light energises the Chi.

Mineral crystals (earth element) have an extraordinary capacity to absorb and expand Chi, so be careful not to put them too near the computer (seek advice from a gemologist).

Place a mineral crystal by your front door if it faces southwest or northeast (enhancing its earth quality).

Keep them clean by rinsing them in water, but do not use salt water as this can apparently damage them.

To understand more about the qualities of the different mineral crystals refer to a specialist book.

CHI, WATER and LANDSCAPE.

Shen Chi – positive Chi . . . Sha chi – negative or cutting Chi.

As Chi passes a sharp corner it begins to spin, forming eddies like on the bend of a fast-flowing river. This energy spin is called cutting Chi and can occur inside or outside a building. If you sit within this field of cutting Chi you tend to feel disoriented. In a room, placement of plants can dissipate it e.g. if you have a square column or a projecting corner, careful placement of a plant at its right angle will interupt these arrows of cutting Chi.

It is better if the path leading to your front door meanders in gentle curves rather than a straight line, thus preventing any potential cutting Chi hitting your entrance door directly.

The driveway or path to your building needs to be wider at the street end and narrower closer to the building, encouraging energy to enter your building.

If a road slopes gently down towards your building, this is considered auspicious as energy is pouring in. Driveways that slope downwards away from your door drain the Chi away. If this is the case for you, direct a light upwards from the bottom of the slope.

In traditional Feng Shui it is considered auspicious to have a hill at the back of your home to shelter your environment and its Chi. In a city the equivalent is having a high-rise building or tall trees behind you.

Chi tends to accumulate around areas of running water, so water is regarded as auspicious.

Water flowing towards your front door brings vitality and money.

Water flowing away from your entrance can carry that vitality away.

Water fountains are popular features especially in the southeast (wealth) and north (career) sectors for abundance. i.e. the impression of life bubbling over.

MORE IN DEPTH INFORMATION FOR YOUR SITE.

IRREGULAR SHAPED BUILDINGS

If your building has an irregular shape (i.e. not square or rectangular as are ideal) then place the main body of the building within the grid and mark the compass directions.

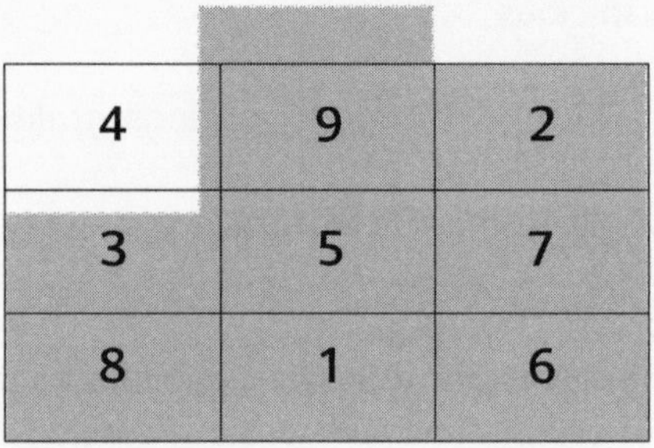

4	9	2
3	5	7
8	1	6

Diagram A

If having superimposed the grid onto your building there are missing sections within the grid, these are called NEGATIVE SPACES. E.g. in diagrams A and B, numbers 4 and 3 have NEGATIVE SPACE. In diagram C, 8 has NEGATIVE SPACE.

Where the building extends beyond the grid, these areas are called POSITIVE SPACES e.g. In diagrams A and B, 9 and 4 have POSITIVE SPACES. In diagram C, number 2 and 6 have POSITIVE SPACE.

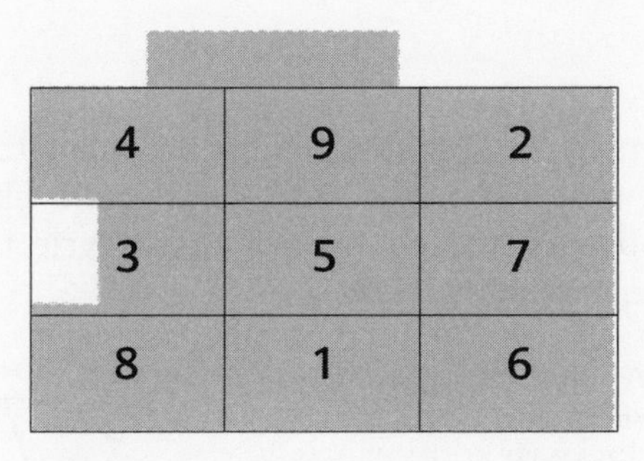

Diagram B

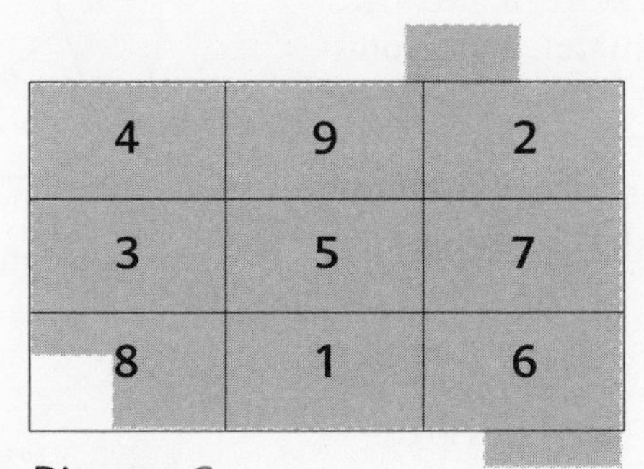

Diagram C

In a correctly placed grid the negative or positive individual SPACES do not exceed 15 per cent of the total site area.

To compensate the NEGATIVE SPACE, emphasise the colours, elements and images etc., that represent those missing areas. These are called cures and are used by practitioners to balance and enhance an environment (See diagram E).

THE CYCLES

The five elements relate to each other according to the following cycles: the natural cycle (using its own elements), the creative or supportive cycle, the exhaustive cycle, the destructive cycle and the mitigating cycle.

THE CREATIVE OR SUPPORTIVE CYCLE OF THE ELEMENTS: This moves in a clockwise motion.
Fire creates earth (ash); under pressure this hardens into metal (minerals); metal under pressure melts, creating liquid (water) through condensation; water feeds wood (plants); wood feeds the burning fire.

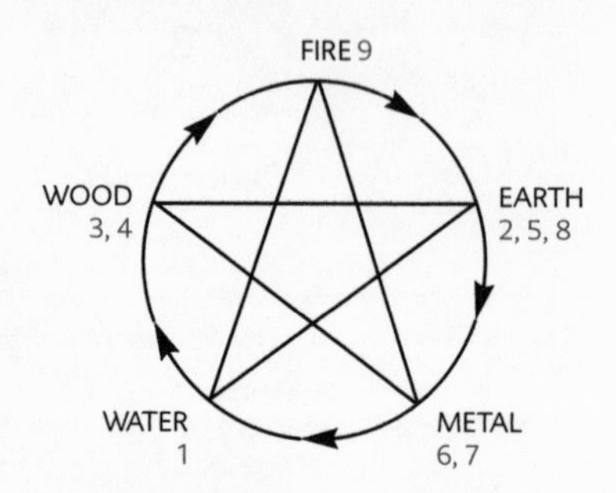

Supportive cycle

THE EXHAUSTIVE CYCLE OF THE ELEMENTS: This moves in an anti-clockwise motion.
Too much fire can burn up all the wood; too much wood can absorb all the water; excess water can rust the metal; metal can transform earth to rock; too much earth (ash) can put out the fire.

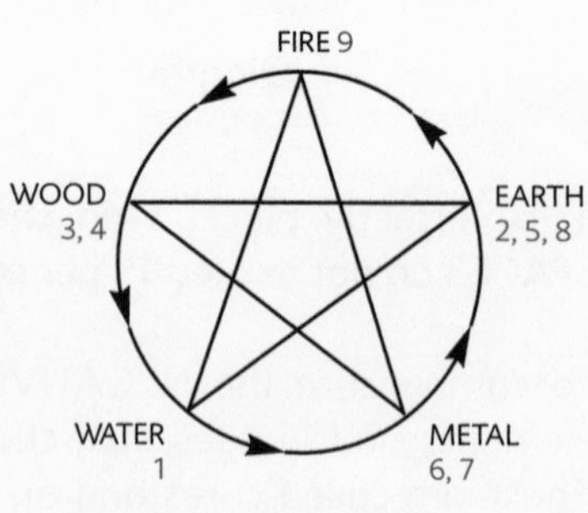

Exhaustive cycle

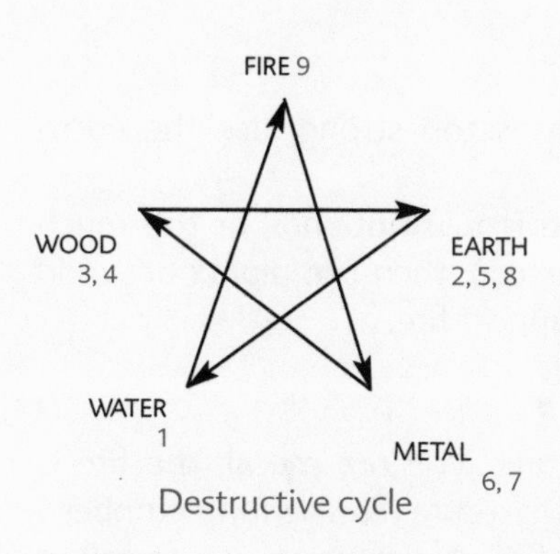

Destructive cycle

THE DESTRUCTIVE CYCLE OF THE ELEMENTS

Life always has its opposite, illustrated here with the arrows of destruction. Fire melts metal; metal cuts wood; wood (roots) spread the earth; earth clogs the water; water can put out the flames.

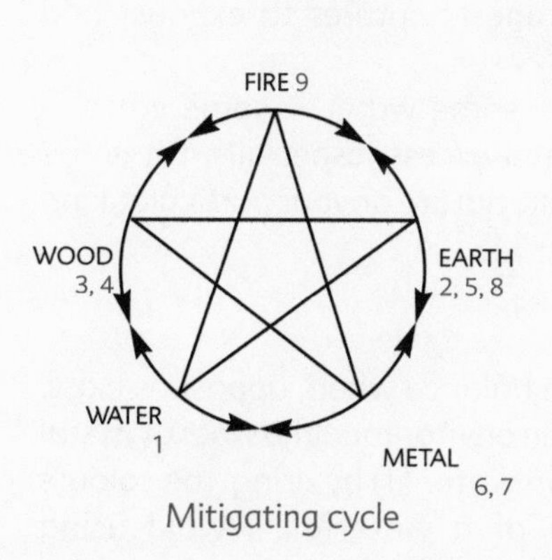

Mitigating cycle

THE MITIGATING CYCLE OF THE ELEMENTS

The mitigating element is the one skipped by the arrows of the destructive cycle.

Earth mitigates fire and metal; metal mitigates water and earth; water mitigates wood and metal; wood mitigates fire and water; fire mitigates wood and earth.

USING THE SUPPORTIVE CYCLE

If you want to stimulate wealth in your life, activate the southeast section (4) using the supportive cycle – introduce the water elements here; the colours for water are black and navy.

USING THE EXHAUSTIVE CYCLE

If excitement and fire (9) energy is too strong, use the earth element or its colours to subdue.
If water element (1) is too strong (too emotional, or too much black/navy and you are a fire person), then use plants or wood elements to exhaust water and support fire.

USING THE DESTRUCTIVE CYCLE

If there is too much fire energy and you are metal, the fire is melting your power, (6 or 7) bring in a cure representing number 1 (water) and this will put out the fire. A picture of a waterfall to destroy the fire would help or stone sculptures to exhaust and subdue it (exhaustive cycle).
We want balance in all things so, some water – some earth – metal – wood – fire – but none in excess, especially if it is the element that undermines your basic nature or your particular kind of business. Use the cures on page 145.

USING THE MITIGATING CYCLE

Use the mitigating cycle to create balance where opposites exist. If the business is finance (4) and the environment has lots of metal (6) (such as steel furniture) bring in water (1) by using the colours black/navy or even an image of a waterfall. (Avoid using representations of the earth element as this clogs water and invigorates metal.)

祝生

If a person whose Kua number is 6 has to work with a 3, it would be good to bring in a 1 to work there or images of water (1). The water mitigates the wood and metal elements.
If your Kua Number is 1 and the room you work is in the southwest (2), and the colour in the room is yellow (earth) and there is a stone floor (earth), bring in metal furniture (6, 7) to subdue the grounding quality of earth and support 1.

If your Kua number is 9 and your door faces West (7), mitigate the energy by painting the door yellow (2).

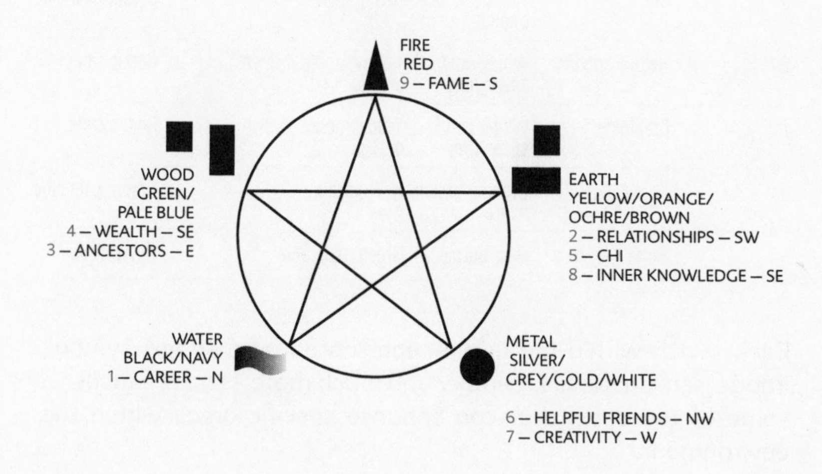

GUIDE FOR ENHANCEMENTS USING THE CYCLES

DIAGRAM D

Area of Lo Shu grid	Area of life	Natural cycle	Creative/supportive cycle	Destructive cycle
1	Career	Navy/black	White, gold, silver, grey	Yellow, ochre, orange brown
2	Relationship	Yellow, ochre	Red, purple	Green, pale blue
3	Ancestors	Green, pale blue	Navy, black	White, gold, silver, grey
4	Wealth	Green, pale blue	Navy, black	White, gold,silver, grey
5	Chi	Yellow, ochre, orange	Red, purple	Green, pale blue
6	Helpful friends	White, gold, silver, grey	Yellow, ochre, brown, orange	Red, purple
7	Creativity	White, gold, silver, grey	Yellow, ochre, brown orange	Red, purple
8	Knowledge	Orange, brown ochre	Red, purple	Green, pale blue
9	Fame	Red, purple	Green, pale blue	Navy, black

Each sector within the grid is represented by a shape, symbol, image, season, family member and much more. Here is a guide to some of the cures that can enhance specific areas within the environment.

DIAGRAM E

AREA OF LO SHU GRID	COMPASS ORIENTATION	ELEMENT	SHAPE	COLOUR (NATURAL CYCLE)	SYMBOLIC REPRESENTATION	AREA OF LIFE
1	NORTH	WATER	ASYMMETRICAL WAVY	BLACK/NAVY	Images of moving water. You don't want stillness here, rather images of what you would love to do: sailing–sking–waterfalls–aquarium–glass–seascapes–paint–mirrors	Career–freedom to do what you want–your journey in life
2	SOUTHWEST	EARTH	SQUARE/FLAT RECTANGLE	YELLOWS OCHRE	Images of union–no images of solitary figures here–photos of union–crystals–cushions–ceramics–flowers–pairs of things	Relationship–platonic, romantic, professional
3	EAST	WOOD	RECTANGLE SQUARE	GREEN PALE BLUE	Images of rising energy–sunrise –tall plants. This represents thunder so music, stereo, piano, television. Wood element–bamboo–family photos	Ancestors–superiors & parents–authority figures
4	SOUTHEAST	WOOD	RECTANGLE SQUARE	GREEN PALE BLUE	Images of rising energy–tall plants. This represents wind–stereo–piano–television. Wood element–bamboo–family photos –gold coins–waterfall –mobile-fans	Wealth & blessings
5	CENTRE	EARTH	SQUARE/FLAT RECTANGLE	YELLOW OCHRE ORANGE	Water in this area should be clean & flowing–crystals–ceramic pots	Chi–health
6	NORTHWEST	STRONG METAL	ROUND/OVAL	SILVER/GOLD WHITE/GREY	Images of support(teachers–gurus)–metal wind chimes	Helpful friends –neighbours, staff, mentors, supporters
7	WEST	LITTLE METAL	ROUND/OVAL	SILVER/GOLD WHITE/GREY	Images of playfulness–children's paintings–sunsets–animals–vase of white flowers–ornaments–lakes–games–metal wind chimes	Creativity–joy inspiration, children
8	NORTHEAST	EARTH	SQUARE/FLAT RECTANGLE	YELLOWS ORANGE OCHRE BROWN	Images of heavy cabinets (represents mountain)–chests –empty boxes–cupboards/drawers–crystal	Inner Knowledge–wisdom
9	SOUTH	FIRE	TRIANGULAR	RED/PURPLE	Inspirational images–lights–candles–images of heroes or painting/sculptures	Fame–illumination in the world

THE TRIGRAMS OF THE PA KUA.

The 8 trigrams of the Pa Kua represent a mathematical pattern of change in the universe and are a combination of Yin and Yang lines.

Yin is represented by a broken line. — —
Yang is represented by a solid line. ——

The eight trigrams were associated with images of nature, family members, the various compass orientations and seasons and were believed to represent the secrets of life and the wisdom of the Universe (see opp. page). These trigrams along with the form of the landscape were the initial building blocks of Feng Shui and they specifically indicate which is the best room for certain usage or for the benefit of particular members of a household.

Four configurations are created by combining them into pairs.

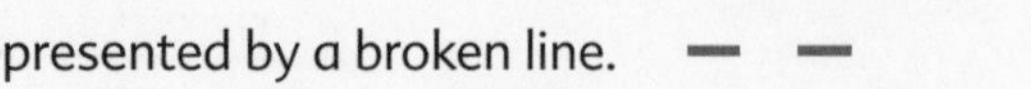

The 8 triagram are created by adding a third line to each of these.

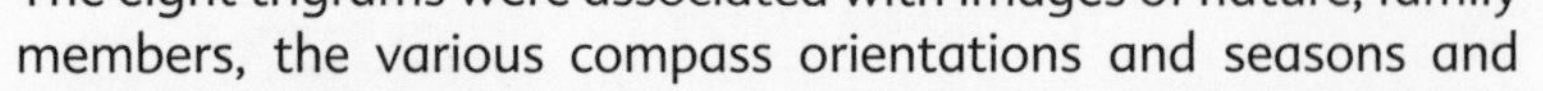

The three lines represent consecutively from top to bottom

HEAVEN
MAN
EARTH

The trigrams were placed in pairs forming what was to later become the 64 hexagrams of the I Ching — an oracle of profound wisdom intended as a guide along one's path in life. This book became a classic and formed the foundation of their philosophical movement, divination, astrology, and of course the continually evolving Feng Shui. The 64 Hexagrams (each consists of 6 either broken or solid lines) and their texts in the I Ching supposedly represent all possible stages of change from birth to death relating to an individual.

K'AN Water

1 Represents career – our journey through life; it is associated with winter; its element is water, its orientation north.

K'UN Earth

2 Represents union and relationships.It is associated with yielding, summer and the maternal female; its element is earth, its orientation southwest.

CHEN Thunder

3 Represents health, vitality, elders, ancestors and family; it is associated with spring and new beginnings; its element is wood. Yang – its orientation east

SUN Wind

4 Represents wealth, blessings, growth and assimilation; it is associated with wind and spring; its element is wood; its orientation southeast.

5 Female number 5 is represented by K'UN Trigram 2.

Male Number 5 is represented by KEN Trigram 8.

CHIEN Heaven

6 Represents leadership, achievement, helpful friends, mentors and teachers – and symbolises heaven; it is associated with the head of the household and autumn; its element is strong metal, its orientation northwest.

TUI Lake

7 Represents creativity, joy, children; it is associated with autumn; its element is little metal, its orientation west.

KEN Mountain

8 Represents inner knowledge, wisdom, quiet – it is associated with winter; its element is earth; its orientation northeast.

LI Fire

9 Represents illumination of self, reputation, visibility (fame) in the world; it is associated with summer; its element is fire its orientation south.

CHARACTER ANALYSIS VIA YOUR ELEMENT AND CHINESE ANIMAL

Your year of birth has an element and a Chinese animal sign. The idea is that you have the qualities of the year and season you were born in. These characteristics influence your compatibility with others, along with the traits of your Chinese animal.

ELEMENT AND PERSONALITY CHARACTERISTICS

WATER:

ELEMENT – This is the part of the cycle where the energy is floating and appears dormant. It is associated with the stillness of winter.
PERSONALITY – Diplomatic, reflective, moody

EARTH:

ELEMENT – Its nature is downward and grounding and it is associated with the settling energy of late summer.
PERSONALITY – Practical and dependable, can be stubborn

WOOD:

ELEMENT – Represents all living things. Its nature is an upward movement of energy and it is associated with the rising energy of springtime.
PERSONALITY – Energetic, born leader , not very good at completing.

METAL:

ELEMENT – Symbolises condensing, inward, consolidating energy and it is associated with the harvest time of autumn.
PERSONALITY – Independent, determined, can be inflexible.

FIRE:

ELEMENT – Its nature is upward and outward, symbolising expansion, burning and heat and it is associated with the active energy of summer.
PERSONALITY – Decisive, passionate, can be vain.

The Star cycle can be used to determine compatibility of the Kua numbers as elements. The numbers within the same element share great commonality and understand each other (natural cycle). Adjacent numbers are very compatible and in romance share great passion. For example, number 4 has great passion and friendship with number 9. Numbers 6 and 7 can share great friendship and even lasting intimacy, though not perhaps with the same passion as adjacent numbers. With opposing numbers there is greater difficulty (following the arrows on the destructive cycle).

The cures described on page 142 can aid relationship difficulty. For example, a number 8 person has to be very careful with a number 3 person. Their opposing differences may cause conflict if they have to live or work together – bring in something or someone representing 9 (mitigating cycle). Numbers 5 and 1: number 1 loses clarity, so this is not a good mix. Use the mitigating cycle and introduce a 6 or 7 person at work or relevant cure. Number 1 (water) finds it hard to be best of friends with a 9 (fire). Water puts out fire. Mitigate with a number 3 or 4 or relevant cure.

ANIMAL SIGN

Each person has good and bad years relative to their personal animal sign and its compatibility with the animal sign of a particular year.

For example, if you are a tiger, you would have had a difficult year in the year of the monkey, 1992, but you would have had a good year in 1990, the year of the horse (see page 63).

ANIMAL CHARACTERISTICS

RAT – Social, ambitious, secretive
OX – Materialistic, reliable, charitable.
TIGER – Sincere, a survivor, reckless
RABBIT – Peaceful, elegant manner, timid.
DRAGON – Loyal, courageous, tending to arrogance.
SNAKE – Profound thinker, gentle cunning, charismatic.
HORSE – Quick witted, popular, can be fickle.
SHEEP – Romantic, honourable,can be a bit negative.
MONKEY – Playful, quick witted, wily.
ROOSTER – Proud, efficient, can be critical.
DOG – Cynical, loyal, cool, independence concealing warmth.
PIG – Kind hearted, resilient, can be superfiicial.

COMPATIBILITY OF ANIMAL SIGNS

The following animal signs are compatible with each other:

RAT – DRAGON – MONKEY
OX – SNAKE – ROOSTER
TIGER – HORSE – DOG
RABBIT – SHEEP – PIG

The following animal signs are the least compatible with each other:

RAT – HORSE
OX – SHEEP
MONKEY – TIGER
DOG – DRAGON
RABBIT – ROOSTER
SNAKE – PIG

Avoid over-stimulating the environment when you attend to the Feng Shui in your home or office during a year representing your incompatable animal.

Your Kua number represents an element on the star cycle and this may differ from the element of your year of birth. A water tiger born in 1962 is a better communicator than a metal tiger born in 1950.

For a female born on 14 September 1953, her element of the year is water, and the element of her Kua number 4 is wood, so she is influenced by both wood and water.

For a male born on 18 March 1947, his element of the year is earth, and the element of his Kua number 8 is earth, so he is doubly influenced by earth characteristics. He would benefit from the metal element in his environment and its related cures (exhaustive cycle) despite initial discomfort.

For a female born on 3 April 1967 her element of the year is fire, and the element of her Kua number 9 is fire, so she is doubly influenced by fire characteristics. She could melt metal personalities (6, 7) and would be uncomfortable in the presence of water characters.

For a male born on 22 July 1961 his element of the year is metal, and the element of his Kua number 3 is wood. His characteristics are influenced by both wood and metal.

GEOPATHIC STRESS.

In addition to being a victim of the elements of wind and water, China experienced hundreds of devastating earthquakes, which contributed no doubt to their need for and evolution of Feng Shui. They believed earthquakes were Chi escaping from under the earth's crust. A fair amount of resulting geopathic stress would have led them to seek a place on the landmass that was balanced; a place of peace on the earth for a building to rest.

Geopathic stress is an area of concern that I did not want to ignore, but surmounting it is not simple. The earth has an electromagnetic field, if there are disturbances in this field generated by underground streams, man-made sewers, main supplies of electricity, water and much more, stress waves are created. Where two waves of stress intercept each other there is resulting geopathic stress. Often these disturbances to the earth can be the result of foundations being dug for buildings, especially where there are major excavations for multi-floor tower blocks in our inner cities. These disturbed areas are normally detected where you find you can sleep on one side of the bed and not the other. Cats often rest where these lines cross. Children often sleep in a certain position on the bed unconsciously attempting to avoid these pathways.

The energy itself isn't bad, it just isn't life enhancing for us humans, though some animals and plants actually thrive in these locations. Your cat may always sleep on your bed for pure comfort, but check it out. You can often recognise these places of stress as places where you find you can't relax despite an ability to do so elsewhere in the same room.

We have electro-magnetic circuits running through our own bodies, and so we are continually affected by our environment externally and internally. Some people who are weakened by illness can find living in a place with geopathic stress especially disturbing.

So how do we find PEACE in an environment with geopathic stress?

It can be visually entertaining for the sceptics and generally interesting to the open-minded to call in an experienced dowser and listen to their opinion. Strategically-placed quartz crystals have been found to be effective in diverting these rays that can penetrate concrete and steel through many floors of a building. Cork floors and linoleum are short-term cures. The long-term view is more difficult, though some 'earth healers' claim to be able to do so.

ELECTRONIC GADGETS.

The above refers to the natural electro-magnetic emanations from the earth. In our environment there are also the artificially created electromagnetic fields radiating from electronic equipment and power cables.

Our electronic gadgets, from computers to microwaves and even digital clocks, give off an excessive amount of electro-magnetic pollution. Although a mild form of this occurs in our natural environments, these electrical gadgets add to it more than is healthy and their field of emanation can extend up to two metres. With your own electrical appliances turn them off at the mains and if you're willing, use a battery radio by your bed at night. There is research currently going on with electricity pylons due to the suspiciously frequent occurance of illnesses in those living nearby.

SICK-BUILDING SYNDROME

Sick-building syndrome is quite different to geopathic stress. Sick buildings are generally the result of inefficient mechanical ventilation systems, fluorescent lights, and fume-emanating equipment.

Some of the new synthetic building materials give off toxic gasses. Often you can smell these when works are newly completed, then after a while you grow accustomed to the smell, though the toxicity has not subsided. Check the ventilation of your environment and endeavour to use non toxic paints and cleaning materials.

For further information there are many books about the healthy home and office.

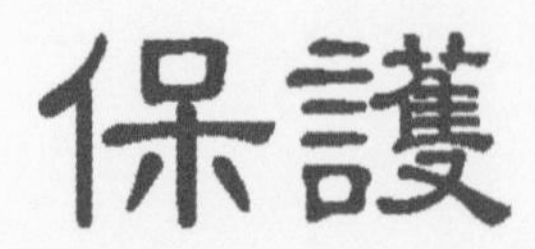

完美的平衡

INNER HOUSE/OUTER HOUSE

As I mentioned earlier, clients sometimes want Feng Shui to change their lives even in areas where they know they have internal psychological blocks. However, moving stuff in the external environment will not necessarily dissolve the equivalent internal psychological furniture. The source of a 'rich' life in all its manifestations is to understand the union and interaction of the two – inner and outer.

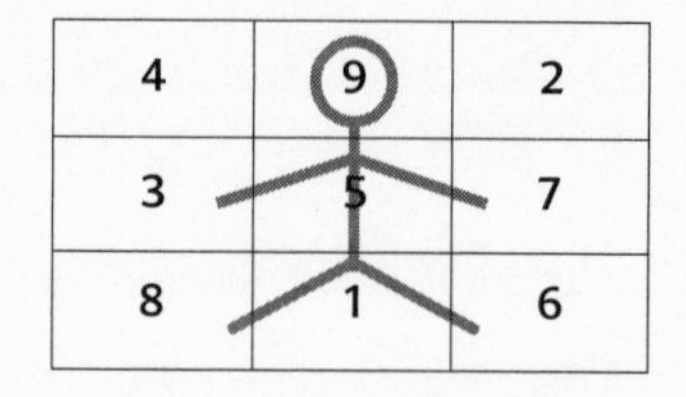

Your environment can reveal a lot about who you are and how you live your life.

That ugly, heavy cupboard you hate sits in the southwest and in life you seem to attract heavy and difficult relationships.

You want your life to get more 'real' yet piles of *Hello* and *O.K!.* magazines fill the northwest location.

The teenager who has always been a handful and is starting to ruin his/her own life and more, has bedroom walls that are covered with the latest horror or violent movie posters generating a hypnotic impact. This is junking up your adolescent's mental computer when it could be better used in a constructive and creative way. Perhaps it is now worryingly reflecting visually and verbally the montage of an unhealthy inner movie screen.

Your future planning never seems to work and your south location is where you shove all that broken equipment that 'one day' (i.e. never) you are going to fix.

This doesn't mean chuck everything and pare down to Zen minimalism and puritanical values – it means get conscious and discern.

So let's have a look at where your inner blocks may relate to your environment and vice versa.

SOUTH, 9 – REPUTATION/RECOGNITION

Helen, a client, expressed a particular wish to enhance the areas of reputation and career. In our consultation she whispered to me in a self-conscious tone: 'I'd really like to have more respect and recognition at work – I'm very good at what I do but, gosh . . . I feel rather conceited saying that.' She had recently resolved to access her reputation via the outer house of Feng Shui, which she had erroneously heard could be a cure all.

In this instance, Feng Shui could definitely benefit her in her environment but it wasn't just external adjustments she needed. Her desire for change was still vulnerable to unconscious self-sabotage. In her formative years modesty was emphasised and heralded as a very noble quality. Now, years later, she has difficulty promoting herself. In her home, her north and south locations were completely cluttered. A profusion of photographs of her domineering parents were displayed throughout and especially in the west – place of play and creativity. I indicated where she had set up the mirroring of her psychological drama in her environment and diplomatically suggested she have a chat with her internal saboteur – the modesty block. Without going into any heavy-duty therapy stuff I suggested a simple technique to help her loosen some of the internal debris. Sometimes just a dialogue with our presenting issue is enough to help us get through to the next level.

The stimulus for this dialogue is to simply ask the presenting issue 'what' questions. For example, using Helen's modesty block, 'What are the pay offs for modesty?' Listen to the answer. Maybe it's 'I get approval' or 'I am a good person'. Ask: 'What do I feel about good people?' Listen to your answer: 'Maybe good people aren't Mammons?' Ask: 'What is uncomfortable about being a Mammon?' 'They are selfish.' Ask: 'What are selfish people like?'

Just keep letting one answer unfold the next question until you have revealed a new perspective or a deeper vision of an old one, then ask as a final question: 'What NEEDS to happen?' The form of the last question is important because instead of being simply investigative like the previous questions, this feeds our NEED and so helps us feel cared for – encouraging a healing. Often when life happens we ask ourselves 'why' questions. But this 'why' form has a subtle aggression to it and just sends us around in ever depressing circles. 'What' used repeatedly has a pragmatism that aids the crystallisation of a new awareness. This technique is simple but remarkably revealing and effective. It can help to simply stop and listen to yourself.

As you release the debris, you begin to feel different and with that, what you then seek from your abode, office and life changes. You've probably had the experience of coming back from a holiday and wanting to de-clutter your space immediately, or to paint it a new colour. A subtle change has occurred internally and you unconsciously want to match it on the outside. The questioning described can give you the opportunity for a quick and painless internal holiday.

Feng Shui is about balance out there and in here.

I don't want to turn this into a therapy book but I thought this simple technique was worth sharing. Either use it by yourself or work with a friend. It is a simple tool to help you be more honest with yourself. Of course, there are many cognitive techniques, but I happen to find this one simple and constructive.

With this information now consider your life and the other aspirations of the Pa Kua.

Southwest	2	Relationship and union
West	7	Creativity and joy
Northwest	6	Helpful friends area
North	1	Career – Your journey in life
Northeast	8	Inner knowledge
East	3	Place of ancestors/ health and wellbeing
Southeast	4	Wealth and Blessings
Centre	5	Chi and health

OUR OUTER HOUSE

+

OUR INNER HOUSE

= REALLY COMING HOME

Hopefully now when you turn the key in the door to your room, you will find yourself opening and entering into a much bigger world.

Working with design I wanted to understand what made a building tick, so for me design for the sake of itself took a back seat. Analysing shape, form, colour, proportion, line, materials, texture, density, light, shade, movement, symbolism, orientation, location, purpose, needs and the influence the space has on our behaviour, desires and outcome was where my passion lay. This may sound like design but it is actually its sponsoring agents.

In a world where design has almost become a lifestyle dictator it helps to understand that the real power lies beyond appearances.

INFORMATION ON SOME OF THE DIFFERENT FENG SHUI SCHOOLS CURRENTLY POPULAR IN THE WEST

CLASSICAL FORM/LANDSCAPE

In this book I have presented the traditional school, which combines the form and compass schools, however, there are those who use the form school independently.

THE JAPANESE 9 STAR KI SCHOOL

Feng Shui orignated in China and crossed the seas to Japan about 2,000 years later in a slightly altered form. This altered state, so the story goes, was apparently due to the fact that some information was actively withheld by the Chinese so as not to divulge their treasured secret. In Japan where they work with the 9 star Ki, males and females are calculated in the tables as if they were the same gender, whereas in China they are treated as interacting opposites, reflecting the duality theory of Yin and Yang. 9 star Ki can be confusing for some females for this reason, as their Kua numbers are quite different from the Chinese tables. Many experts whose experience and understanding originated in the study of macrobiotics use this method for character analysis especially relevant for diet.

FLYING STAR – Time and space Feng Shui

Flying Star was intended as a form of divination, for calculating lucky periods for transactions and the like.

I have been given to understand that many of the complex tabulated calculations used by various experts on this method differ. This is due to the fact that many of the original tables were destroyed, during the revolution by Mao Zedong. After that period in Chinese history, much of the information was by memory and word of mouth. Considering the complexity of the tables, bar the first two stages which are straightforward, many scholars have expressed concern that some of those in use today are for Yin burial sites and not for the dwelling Yang sites they are being applied to. Since I have no way of comfortably discerning the correct tables where even great scholars disagree, for me flying star flies out the window. Some experts may have discovered authentic sources, you must question and discern.

BLACK HAT SECT

The Black Hat Sect was developed in America about fifteen years ago by Thomas Lin Yun. Similar to Intuitive Feng Shui it has a fixed grid. It is rather more mystically and superstitiously based than any of the above as it applies principles of Tibetan Buddhism. Member consultants tend to follow their Mentor Lin Yun.

INTUITIVE FENG SHUI

Intuitive Feng Shui is a method that has evolved in the West over the last fifteen to twenty years. This has no formal guidelines other than a fixed grid which, for example, proposes that the area supporting relationships will always be to the far right corner as you enter any environment, whichever side of the street you live, as opposed to it always being located in the southwest as in the Compass school. Beyond this fixed grid the consultant applies their intuition and knowledge.

How can you measure their expertise? Well that would require that they come recommended and that you hone your discernment.

• • •

If you decide to call in a consultant who hasn't come by recommendation, prepare a list of pertinent questions and discuss your needs with him or her. Most experienced consultants expect to have an initial discussion before confirming an appointment.

SELF HELP FENG SHUI

If this book helps you in balancing your own environment . . . great . . . but before you consider helping someone else with your new skills, go on a study course. This book is just a very small window into a multi-faceted subject and a deeper understanding is needed before becoming a professional. Understanding ourselves in our own environment is one thing, influencing someone else is quite a different responsibility.

It is hard to learn from a book, experience is your best teacher. But a book will help you to ask your consultant more exacting questions and may inspire further study.

We and our planet are much much more than we seem.

Enjoy the journey.

Rosalyn Dexter came to feng shui from a background in art and architecture and a successful career in property development and design. Realising that she had unconsciously been using many of its principles in her most successful buildings, she developed her knowledge of the subject and trained with many respected masters. Along the way she investigated other Eastern practices and grew a deep understanding of man in his environment.

Rosalyn continues to consult in building development and design often acting as a bridge between client and architect, as well as carrying out feng shui consultations for a range of high-profile personal and company clients.

IF YOU HAVE ANY QUESTIONS OR SUGGESTIONS REGARDING INFORMATION IN THIS BOOK, PLEASE FORWARD THEM TO PO BOX 21263, LONDON W9 1YU

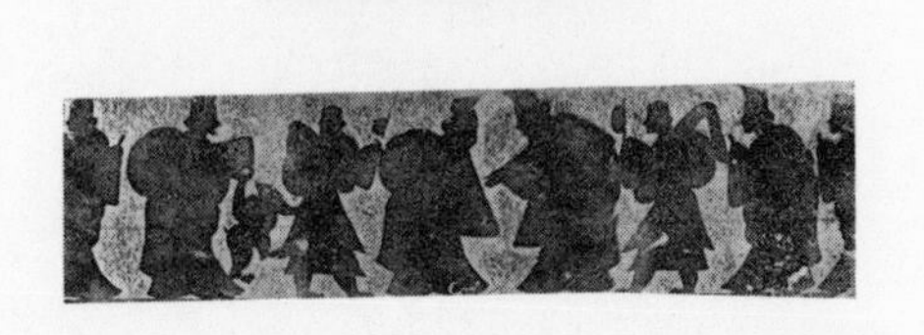

祝生